AMERICA PERCEIVED:

A View from Abroad
in the 19th Century

AMERICA PERCEIVED

AMERICA PERCEIVED:
A View from Abroad
in the 19th Century

Edited by

William J. Baker

Series Editor
James Axtell

Pendulum Press, Inc.

West Haven, Connecticut   El Monte, California

Clothbound Edition   *ISBN 0-88301-144-1*   *Complete Set*
        0-88301-147-6   *This Volume*

Paperback Edition   *ISBN 0-88301-123-9*   *Complete Set*
        0-88301-126-3   *This Volume*

Library of Congress Catalog Card Number   73-94109

Published by
Pendulum Press, Inc.
An Academic Industries, Inc. Company
The Academic Building
Saw Mill Road
West Haven, Connecticut 06516

Printed in the United States of America

CONTENTS

ABOUT THE EDITOR

William J. Baker received his undergraduate degree from Furman University, and a B.D. from Southeastern Seminary. He attended the University of Zurich and Duke University and later received a Ph.D. in history from Cambridge University. At present he is Associate Professor of history at the University of Maine at Orono. He has written numerous articles which have been published in journals, reviews, and magazines.

ABOUT THE SERIES EDITOR

James Axtell, after receiving his B.A. from Yale University, went on to study at Oxford International Summer School, and later received his Ph.D. from Cambridge University. Mr. Axtell has taught at Yale University and currently is Associate Professor of history at Sarah Lawrence College. He has published many articles, reviews, and essays and has served as general editor of several educational publications. He is the author of the forthcoming book, *The School upon a Hill: Education and Society in Colonial New England.*

FOREWORD

> Oh wad some power the giftie gie us
> To see ourselves as others see us!
> It wad frae monie a blunder free us,
>   An' foolish notion.
> Robert Burns, "To a Louse" (1786)

AMERICA PERCEIVED was created as a companion to THE AMERICAN PEOPLE series and as an independent collection of primary sources for the study of American history. Like its companion, it is founded on the belief that the study of history in the schools and junior levels of college generally begins at the wrong end. That study usually begins with abstract and pre-digested *conclusions*—the conclusions of other historians as filtered through the pen of a textbook writer—and not with the primary sources of the past and unanswered *questions* —the starting place of the historian himself.

Since we all need, use, and think about the past in our daily lives, we are all historians. The question is whether we can be skillful, accurate, and useful historians. The only way to become such is to exercise our historical skills and interests until we gain competence. But we have to exercise them in the same ways the best historians do or we will be kidding ourselves that we are *doing* history when in fact we are only absorbing sponge-like the results of someone else's historical competence.

Historical competence must begin with one crucial skill—the ability to distinguish between past and present. Without a sharp sense of the past as a different time from our own, we will be unable to accord the people of the past the respect that we would like to receive from the people of the future. And without according them that respect, we will be unable to recognize their integrity as individuals or to understand them as human beings like ourselves.

A good sense of the past depends primarily on a good sense of the present, on experience, and on the imaginative empathy to relate ourselves to human situations not our own. Since most students have had a relatively brief experience of life and have not yet given full expression to their imaginative sympathies, THE AMERICAN PEOPLE was designed to draw upon the one essential prerequisite for the study of history that all students possess—the lives they have lived from birth to young adulthood. It asked us to look at the American experience from the *inside*, through the eyes of the participants who lived through the American life cycles, with the understanding gained from living through our own. AMERICA PERCEIVED seeks to draw more upon our imaginative sympathy by asking us to look at America from the *outside*, through the eyes of visitors, travellers, and critics whose lives and values were very different from those of the Americans they saw.

One view (inside or outside) is not necessarily better—that is, more accurate, sensitive, objective, complete—than the other. Both views are necessary to take the full measure of the country in all its complexity. The value of the view ultimately depends upon the observer. The quality of a foreigner's observations depends less upon his initial attitude toward America than upon his personal qualities—his objectivity, breadth of vision, accuracy of perception, sensitivity to human character, and tolerance of cultural difference. For example, although a perceptive visitor may come to America expecting the worst, his observations may be of great value because he can accurately see some of the country's dark spots and contradictions that perhaps remain hidden to Americans or to other visitors who come expecting only the best. On the other hand, the observations of an insensitive visitor who comes expecting the best may be of small value because he is too accepting of what well-meaning Americans tell him or because he is unable to see the country's faults and contradictions as well as its more obvious strengths and consistencies.

Foreign observers possess one quality that gives special value to their views of America: their foreignness. They are the products of different cultures which do not share all the assumptions, values, and standards of Americans. They see the world differently than Americans because they have been taught by their culture to see the world differently. In any culture there are aspects of life—they may be good or bad—which for some reason its own members are either unable to see or take so much for granted that they are never mentioned. But few cultures develop exactly the same blind spots about the same aspects of life. Consequently, the visiting members of one culture may be able to see those unrecognized or unmentioned aspects of another culture simply because they are used to seeing them—or not seeing them as the case may be—in their own culture. It is this angle of vision that gives the perceptions of foreigners their primary historical value.

But foreigners' observations usually have one built-in limitation: they are static snapshots of America frozen in time. Because of their relatively short stay, travellers seldom capture a full view of the historical development of the country that made it what it is when they see it. They record only the end product of a long process. Of course curiosity, historical research, and a good interviewing technique can overcome some of this limitation, but they can seldom erase it completely. Consequently, to gain an idea of historical change—as well as stability—we must place these snapshots in chronological order and compare them. This is sometimes difficult because travellers may not focus upon comparable subjects in successive periods, but in general the same range of subjects will capture visitors' interest, especially in a period of moderate or slow change. Visitors are adept at avoiding fads.

Since the experience of each student is the only prerequisite for the study of primary sources at the first level, annotations and introductory material have been reduced to a minimum, simply enough to identify the sources, their authors, and the circumstances in which they were written.

But the remains of the past are mute by themselves. Many sources have survived that can tell us what happened in the past and why, but they have to be questioned properly to reveal their secrets. So by way of illustration, a number of questions have been asked in each chapter, but these should be supplemented by the students whose experiences and knowledge and interests are, after all, the flywheel of the educational process. Although the questions and sources are divided into chapters, they should be used freely in the other chapters;

the collection should be treated as a whole. And although most of the illustrative questions are confined to the sources at hand, questions that extend to the present should be asked to anchor the acquired knowledge of the past in the immediate experience of the present. Only then will learning be real and lasting and history brought to life.

INTRODUCTION

Ever since the day Christopher Columbus returned to Europe with the news of riches to be exploited and natives to be converted, European visitors to America have been eager to publish their views of the New World. By the nineteenth century, travel accounts, diaries, and volumes of letters from European travelers in America poured from the press. The New World was no longer merely a place that offered raw materials and free land, exotic natives and colonial settlements. It was the seat of democracy, a new, bold experiment in the affairs of modern civilization.

The contrast with the Old World was dramatic. In Europe hereditary monarchs still reigned, supported by an aristocratic tradition and state religions which controlled education. No physical, unclaimed frontiers existed. Society was highly class-structured, and few Europeans thought seriously in terms of social equality. Families were paternalistic, with women and children assumed to be subservient to the man. At every point this prior cultural conditioning of the European visitor ran headlong against American ideas and institutions.

Whereas some travelers were willing merely to report on what they saw, most were trying to prevent or to encourage the transmission of the American perspective to Europe. As Alexis de Tocqueville, a Frenchman who came to the United States in the 1830s, admitted candidly, most Europeans came "to find instruction by which we ourselves may profit." They found that democracy was not simply a political system. Based on philosophical and religious assumptions concerning the nature of man, the good life, and society, democracy resulted in the re-ordering of familial relationships, educational priorities, and economic enterprise.

James Bryce, an Englishman who visited America several times in the late nineteenth century, spoke for hundreds of European observers when he referred to "the incomparable significance of the American experience." As the American democratic experience continues to be important in the course of human affairs, we would do well to consider its origins, its strengths and limitations, and its future tendencies as seen through the eyes of others.

I. DEMOCRACY IN AMERICA: A COMPREHENSIVE VIEW

In the early years of the nineteenth century, European travelers were primarily from the upper classes, for only they could afford the high cost and time involved in a trip across the Atlantic..With few exceptions they were highly critical of American democracy. In their view, the idea of equality which lay at the base of democracy was potentially destructive of all the laws, order, and traditional values on which western civilization was built.

One observer who attempted to present a balanced assessment of American democracy was Alexis de Tocqueville, a young liberal French aristocrat who visited the United States in 1831. His *Democracy in America* (4 vols., Paris, 1835-1840), captured the imagination of the English-speaking world. Americans themselves read it to better understand themselves, and Englishmen read it in order to comprehend the present condition and future tendencies of their rebellious cousins across the sea. According to de Tocqueville, what was the place of law in a democracy? Why did American democracy prosper despite poor leaders? What was the source of America's "irritable patriotism"? In what aspects of American life was a "tyranny of the majority" at work?

The following passages from Democracy in America *are taken from a translation by Henry Reeve (London, 1862), vol. 1, pp. 276-79, 282-85, 298-301, 309-10.*

13

The defects and the weaknesses of a democratic government may very readily be discovered; they are demonstrated by the most flagrant instances, whilst its beneficial influence is less perceptibly exercised. A single glance suffices to detect its evil consequences, but its good qualities can only be discerned by long observation. The Laws of the American democracy are frequently defective or incomplete; they sometimes attack vested rights, or give a sanction to others which are dangerous to the community; but even if they were good, the frequent changes which they undergo would be an evil. How comes it, then, that the American republics prosper, and maintain their position?

In the consideration of laws, a distinction must be carefully observed between the end at which they aim, and the means by which they are directed to that end; between their absolute, and their relative excellence. If it be the intention of the legislator to favour the interests of the minority at the expense of the majority, and if the measures he takes are so combined as to accomplish the object he has in view with the least possible expense of time and exertion, the law may be well drawn up, although its purpose be bad; and the more efficacious it is, the greater is the mischief which it causes.

Democratic laws generally tend to promote the welfare of the greatest possible number; for they emanate from the majority of the citizens, who are subject to error, but who cannot have an interest opposed to their own advantage. The laws of an aristocracy tend, on the contrary, to concentrate wealth and power in the hands of the minority, because an aristocracy, by its very nature, constitutes a minority. It may therefore be asserted, as a general proposition, that the purpose of a democracy in the conduct of its legislation, is useful to a greater number of citizens, than that of an aristocracy. This is, however, the sum total of its advantages.

Aristocracies are infinitely more expert in the science of legislation than democracies ever can be. They are possessed of a self-control which protects them from the errors of temporary excitement; and they form lasting designs which they mature with the assistance of favourable opportunities. Aristocratic government proceeds with the dexterity of art; it understands how to make the collective force of all its laws converge at the same time to a given point. Such is not the case with democracies, whose laws are almost always ineffective or inopportune. The means of democracy are therefore more imperfect than those of aristocracy, and the measures which it unwittingly adopts are frequently opposed to its own cause; but the object it has in view is more useful.

Let us now imagine a community so organized by nature, or by its constitution, that it can support the transitory action of bad laws, and that it can await, without destruction, the general tendency of the legislation: we shall then be able to conceive that a democratic government, notwithstanding its defects, will be most fitted to conduce to the prosperity of this community. This is precisely what has occurred in the United States; and I repeat, what I have before remarked, that the great advantage of the Americans consists in their being able to commit faults which they may afterwards repair.

An analogous observation may be made respecting public officers. It is easy to perceive that the American democracy frequently errs in the choice of the individuals to whom it entrusts the power of the administration; but it is more difficult to say why the State prospers under their rule. In the first place it is to be remarked, that if in a democratic State the governors have less honesty and less capacity than elsewhere, the governed on the other hand are more enlightened and more attentive to their interests. As the people in democracies is more incessantly vigilant in its affairs, and more jealous of its rights, it prevents its representatives from abandoning that general line of conduct which its own interest prescribes. In the second place it must be remembered that if the democratic magistrate is more apt to misuse his power, he possesses it for a shorter period of time. But there is yet another reason which is still more general and conclusive. It is no doubt of importance to the welfare of nations that they should be governed by men of talents and virtue; but it is perhaps still more important that the interests of those men should not differ from the interests of the community at large; for if such were the case, virtues of a high order might become useless, and talents might be turned to a bad account. I say that it is important that the interests of the persons in authority should not conflict with or oppose the interests of the community at large; but I do not insist upon their having the same interests as the *whole* population, because I am not aware that such a state of things ever existed in any country.

No political form has hitherto been discovered, which is equally favourable to the prosperity and the development of all the classes into which society is divided. These classes continue to form, as it were, a certain number of distinct nations in the same nation; and experience has shown that it is no less dangerous to place the fate of these classes exclusively in the hands of any one of them, than it is to make one people the arbiter of the destiny of another. When the rich alone govern, the interest of the poor is always endangered; and when the poor make the laws, that of the rich incurs very serious risks. The advantage of democracy does not consist, therefore, as has sometimes been asserted, in favouring the prosperity of all, but simply in contributing to the well-being of the greatest possible number. . . .

There is one sort of patriotic attachment which principally arises from that instinctive, disinterested and undefinable feeling which connects the affections of man with his birthplace. This natural fondness is united to a taste for ancient customs, and to a reverence for ancestral traditions of the past; those who cherish it love their country as they love the mansion of their fathers. They enjoy the tranquillity which it affords them; they cling to the peaceful habits which they have contracted within its bosom; they are attached to the reminiscences which it awakens, and they are even pleased by the state of obedience in which they are placed. This patriotism is sometimes stimulated by religious enthusiasm, and then it is capable of making the most prodigious efforts. It is in itself a kind of religion: it does not reason, but it acts from the impulse of faith and of sentiment. By some nations the monarch has been regarded as a personification of the country; and the fervour of patriotism being converted into the fervour of loyalty, they took a sympathetic pride in his conquests, and gloried in his power. At one time, under the ancient monarchy, the French felt a sort of satisfaction in the sense of their dependence upon the arbitrary pleasure of their king, and they were wont to say with pride, "We are the subjects of the most powerful king in the world."

But, like all instinctive passions, this kind of patriotism is more apt to prompt transient exertion, than to supply the motives of continuous endeavour. It may save the State in critical circumstances, but it will not unfrequently allow the nation to decline in the midst of peace. Whilst the manners of a people are simple, and its faith unshaken; whilst society is steadily based upon traditional institutions, whose legitimacy has never been contested, this instinctive patriotism is wont to endure.

But there is another species of attachment to a country which is more rational than the one we have been describing. It is perhaps less generous and less ardent, but it is more fruitful and more lasting; it is coeval with the spread of knowledge, it is nurtured by the laws, it is confounded with the personal interest of the citizen. A man comprehends the influence which the prosperity of his country has upon his own welfare; he is aware that the laws authorize him to contribute his assistance to that prosperity, and he labours to promote it as a portion of his interest in the first place, and as a portion of his right in the second. . . .

In the United States, the inhabitants were thrown but as yesterday upon the soil which they now occupy, and they brought neither customs nor traditions with them there; they meet each other for the first time with no previous acquaintance; in short, the instinctive love of their country can scarcely exist in their minds; but every one takes as zealous an interest in the affairs of his township, his county, and of the whole State, as if they were his own, because every one, in his sphere, takes an active part in the government of society.

The lower orders in the United States are alive to the perception of the influence exercised by the general prosperity upon their own welfare; and simple as this observation is, it is one which is but too rarely made by the people. But in America the people regards this prosperity as the result of its own exertions; the citizen looks upon the fortune of the public as his private interest, and he cooperates in its success, not so much from a sense of pride or of duty, as from, what I shall venture to term, cupidity.

It is unnecessary to study the institutions and the history of the Americans in order to discover the truth of this remark, for their manners render it sufficiently evident. As the American participates in all that is done in his country, he thinks himself obliged to defend whatever may be censured; for it is not only his country which is attached upon these occasions, but it is himself. The consequence is, that his national pride resorts to a thousand artifices, and to all the petty tricks of individual vanity.

Nothing is more embarrassing in the ordinary intercourse of life, than this irritable patriotism of the Americans. A stranger may be very well inclined to praise many of the institutions of their country, but he begs permission to blame some of the peculiarities which he observes,—a permission which is however inexorably refused. America is therefore a free country, in which, lest anybody should be hurt by your remarks, you are not allowed to speak freely of private individuals or of the State; of the citizens or of the authorities; of public or of private undertakings, or, in short, of anything at all, except it be of the climate and the soil; and even then Americans will be found ready to defend either the one or the other as if they had been contrived by the inhabitants of the country.

In our times, option must be made between the patriotism of all and the government of a few; for the force and activity which the first confers, are irreconcilable with the guarantees of tranquillity which the second furnishes. . . .

It is not always feasible to consult the whole people, either directly or indirectly, in the formation of the law; but it cannot be denied that when such a measure is possible, the authority of the law is very much augmented. This popular origin, which impairs the excellence and the wisdom of legislation, contributes prodigiously to increase its power. There is an amazing strength in the expression of the determination of a whole people; and when it declares itself, the imagination of those who are most inclined to contest it, is overawed by its authority. The truth of this fact is very well known by parties; and they consequently strive to make out a majority whenever they can. If they have not the greater numbers of voters on their side, they assert that the true majority abstained from voting; and if they are foiled even there, they have recourse to the body of those persons who had no votes to give.

In the United States, except slaves, servants, and paupers in the receipt of relief from the townships, there is no class of persons who do not exercise the elective franchise, and who do not indirectly contribute to make the laws. Those who design to attack the laws must consequently either modify the opinion of the nation or trample upon its decision.

A second reason, which is still more weighty, may be further adduced; in the United States every one is personally interested in enforcing the obedience of the whole community to the law; for as the minority may shortly rally the majority to its principles, it is interested in professing that respect for the decrees of the legislator, which it may soon have occasion to claim for its own. However irksome an enactment may be, the citizen of the United States complies with it, not only because it is the work of the majority, but because it originates in his own authority; and he regards it as a contract to which he is himself a party.

In the United States, then, that numerous and turbulent multitude does not exist, which always looks upon the law as its natural enemy, and accordingly surveys it with fear and with distrust. It is impossible, on the other hand, not to perceive that all classes display the utmost reliance upon the legislation of their country, and that they are attached to it by a kind of parental affection.

I am wrong, however, in saying all classes; for as in America the European scale of authority is inverted, the wealthy are there placed in a position analogous to that of the poor in the Old World, and it is the opulent classes which frequently look upon the law with suspicion. I have already observed that the advantage of democracy is not, as has been sometimes asserted, that it protects the interests of the whole community, but simply that it protects those of the majority. In the United States, where the poor rule, the rich have always some reason to dread the abuses of their power. This natural anxiety of the rich may produce a sullen dissatisfaction, but society is not disturbed by it; for, the same reason which induces the rich to withhold their confidence in the legislative authority, makes them obey its mandates: their wealth, which prevents them from making the law, prevents them from withstanding it. Amongst civilized nations revolts are rarely excited except by such persons as have nothing to lose by them; and if the laws of a democracy are not always worthy of respect, at least they always obtain it: for those who usually infringe the laws have no excuse for not complying with the enactments they have themselves made, and by which they are themselves benefited, whilst the citizens whose interests might be promoted by the infraction of them, are induced, by their character and their station, to submit to the decisions of the legislature, whatever they may be. Besides which, the people in America obeys the law not only because it emanates from the popular authority, but because that authority may modify it in any points which may prove vexatory; a law is observed because it is a self-imposed evil in the first place, and an evil of transient duration in the second. . . .

The very essence of democratic government consists in the absolute sovereignty of the majority; for there is nothing in democratic states which is capable of resisting it. . . .

The legislature is, of all political institutions, the one which is most easily swayed by the wishes of the majority. The Americans determined that the members of the legislature should be elected by the people immediately, and for a very brief term, in order to subject them, not only to the general convictions, but even to the daily passions of their constituents. The members of both Houses are taken from the same class in society, and are nominated in the same manner; so that the modifications of the legislative bodies are almost as rapid and quite as irresistible as those of a single assembly. It is to a legislature thus constituted, that almost all the authority of the government has been entrusted.

But whilst the law increased the strength of those authorities which of themselves were strong, it enfeebled more and more those which were naturally weak. It deprived the representatives of the executive of all stability and independence; and by subjecting them completely to the caprices of the legislature, it robbed them of the slender influence which the nature of a democratic government might have allowed them to retain. In several States, the judicial power was also submitted to the elective discretion of the majority; and in all of them its existence was made to depend on the pleasure of the legislative authority, since the representatives were empowered annually to regulate the stipend of the judges.

Custom, however, has done even more than law. A proceeding which will in the end set all the guarantees of representative government at naught, is becoming more and more general in the United States: it frequently happens that the electors, who choose a delegate, point out·a certain line of conduct to him, and impose upon him a certain number of positive obligations which he is pledged to fulfil. With the exception of the tumult, this comes to the same thing as if the majority of the populace held its deliberations in the market-place.

Several other circumstances concur in rendering the power of the majority in America not only preponderant, but irresistible. The moral authority of the majority is partly based upon the notion, that there is more intelligence and more wisdom in a great number of men collected together than in a single individual, and that the quantity of legislators is more important than their quality. The theory of equality is in fact applied to the intellect of man; and human pride is thus assailed in its last retreat, by a doctrine which the minority hesitate to admit, and in which they very slowly concur. Like all other powers, and perhaps more than all other powers, the authority of the many requires the sanction of time; at first it enforces obedience by constraint; but its laws are not respected until they have long been maintained.

The right of governing society, which the majority supposes itself to derive from its superior intelligence, was introduced into the United States by the first settlers; and this idea, which would be sufficient of itself to create a free nation, has now been amalgamated with the manners of the people, and the minor incidents of social intercourse.

The French, under the old monarchy, held it for a maxim, (which is still a fundamental principle of the English Constitution), that the King could do no wrong; and if he did do wrong, the blame was imputed to his advisers. This notion was highly favourable to habits of obedience; and it enabled the subject to complain of the law, without ceasing to love and honour the lawgiver. The Americans entertain the same opinion with respect to the majority.

The moral power of the majority is founded upon yet another principle, which is, that the interests of the many are to be preferred to those of the few. It will readily be perceived that the respect here professed for the rights of the majority must naturally increase or diminish according to the state of parties. When a nation is divided into several irreconcilable factions, the privilege of the majority is often overlooked, because it is intolerable to comply with its demands.

If there existed in America a class of citizens whom the legislating majority sought to deprive of exclusive privileges, which they had possessed for ages, and to bring down from an elevated station to the level of the ranks of the multitude, it is probable that the minority would be less ready to comply with its laws. But as the United States were colonized by men holding equal rank amongst themselves, there is as yet no natural or permanent source of dissension between the interests of its different inhabitants.

There are certain communities in which the persons who constitute the minority can never hope to draw over the majority to their side, because they must then give up the very point which is at issue between them. Thus, an aristocracy can never become a majority whilst it retains its exclusive privileges, and it cannot cede its privileges without ceasing to be an aristocracy.

In the United States, political questions cannot be taken up in so general and absolute a manner; and all parties are willing to recognize the rights of the majority, because they all hope to turn those rights to their own advantage at some future time. The majority therefore in that country exercises a prodigious actual authority, and a moral influence which is scarcely less preponderant; no obstacles exist which can impede, or so much as retard its progress, or which can induce it to heed the complaints of those whom it crushes upon its path. This state of things is fatal in itself and dangerous for the future. . . .

It is in the examination of the display of public opinion in the United States, that we clearly perceive how far the power of the majority surpasses all the powers with which we are acquainted in Europe. Intellectual principles exercise an influence which is so invisible and often so inappreciable, that they baffle the toils of oppression. At the present time the most absolute monarchs in Europe are unable to prevent certain notions, which are opposed to their authority, from circulating in secret throughout their dominions, and even in their courts. Such is not the case in America; as long as the majority is still undecided, discussion is carried on; but as soon as its decision is irrevocably pronounced, a submissive silence is observed; and the friends, as well as the opponents, of the measure, unite in assenting to its propriety. The reason of this is perfectly clear: no monarch is so absolute as to combine all the powers of society in his own hands, and to conquer all opposition, with the energy of a majority, which is invested with the right of making and of executing the laws.

The authority of a king is purely physical, and it controls the actions of the subject without subduing his private will; but the majority possesses a power which is physical and moral at the same time; it acts upon the will as well as upon the actions of men, and it represses not only all contest, but all controversy.

I know no country in which there is so little true independence of mind and freedom of discussion as in America. In any constitutional state in Europe every sort of religious and political theory may be advocated and propagated abroad; for there is no country in Europe so subdued by any single authority, as not to contain citizens who are ready to protect the man who raises his voice in the cause of truth, from the consequences of his hardihood. If he is unfortunate enough to live under an absolute government, the people is upon his side; if he inhabits a free country, he may find a shelter behind the authority of the throne, if he require one. The aristocratic part of society supports him in some countries, and the democracy in others. But in a nation where democratic institutions exist, organized like those of the United States, there is but one sole authority, one single element of strength and of success, with nothing beyond it.

II. HOME, WOMEN, AND CHILDREN

In the Old World the home served as the foundation and training ground for a class-structured social order with definite authority figures; the American home appeared to be based on, and to encourage, equality. In what ways were American women and children equal to men? What were the sources of this equality? How did American women differ from European women? Why were American children so precocious? How did the mania for business success affect the home? Who was the effective head of the American household?

Alexis de Tocqueville's Democracy in America *analyzed, among other things, "The Influence of Democracy on Manners" in antebellum America. The following observations on the democratic family and the equality of the sexes are taken from the Henry Reeve Translation of 1862 (London), vol. 2, pp. 229-236, 251-255.*

It has been universally remarked, that in our time the several members of a family stand upon an entirely new footing towards each other; that the distance which formerly separated a father from his sons has been lessened; and that paternal authority, if not destroyed, is at least impaired.

Something analogous to this, but even more striking, may be observed in the United States. In America the family, in the Roman and aristocratic signification of the word, does not exist. All that remains of it are a few vestiges in the first years of childhood, when the father exercises, without opposition, that absolute domestic author-

24

ity, which the feebleness of his children renders necessary, and which their interest, as well as his own incontestable superiority, warrants. But as soon as the young American approaches manhood,. the ties of filial obedience are relaxed day by day: master of his thoughts, he is soon master of his conduct. In America there is, strictly speaking, no adolescence: at the close of boyhood the man appears, and begins to trace out his own path.

It would be an error to suppose that this is preceded by a domestic struggle, in which the son has obtained by a sort of moral violence the liberty that his father refused him. The same habits, the same principles which impel the one to assert his independence, predispose the other to consider the use of that independence as an incontestable right. The former does not exhibit any of those rancorous or irregular passions which disturb men long after they have shaken off an established authority; the latter feels none of that bitter and angry regret which is apt to survive a by-gone power. The father foresees the limits of his authority long beforehand, and when the time arrives he surrenders it without a struggle: the son looks forward to the exact period at which he will be his own master; and he enters upon his freedom without precipitation and without effort, as a possession which is his own and which no one seeks to wrest from him.

It may perhaps not be without utility to show how these changes which take place in family relations, are closely connected with the social and political revolution which is approaching its consummation under our own observation.

There are certain great social principles, which a people either introduces everywhere, or tolerates nowhere. In countries which are aristocratically constituted with all the gradations of rank, the government never makes a direct appeal to the mass of the governed: as men are united together, it is enough to lead the foremost,—the rest will follow. This is equally applicable to the family, as to all aristocracies which have a head.

Amongst aristocratic nations, social institutions recognize, in truth, no one in the family but the father; children are received by society at his hands; society governs him, he governs them. Thus the parent has not only a natural right, but he acquires a political right, to command them: he is the author and the support of his family; but he is also its constituted ruler.

In democracies, where the government picks out every individual singly from the mass, to make him subservient to the general laws of the community, no such intermediate person is required: a father is there, in the eye of the law, only a member of the community, older and richer than his sons.

When most of the conditions of life are extremely unequal, and the inequality of these conditions is permanent, the notion of a superior grows upon the imaginations of men: if the law invested him with no privileges, custom and public opinion would concede them. When, on the contrary, men differ but little from each other, and do not always remain in dissimilar conditions of life, the general notion of a superior becomes weaker and less distinct: it is vain for legislation to strive to place him who obeys very much beneath him who commands; the manners of the time bring the two men nearer to one another, and draw them daily towards the same level.

Although the legislation of an aristocratic people should grant no peculiar privileges to the heads of families, I shall not be the less convinced that their power is more respected and more extensive than in a democracy; for I know that, whatsoever the laws may be, superiors always appear higher and inferiors lower in aristocracies than amongst democratic nations.

When men live more for the remembrance of what has been than for the care of what is, and when they are more given to attend to what their ancestors thought than to think themselves, the father is the natural and necessary tie between the past and the present—the link by which the ends of these two chains are connected. In aristocracies, the oracle of its traditions, the expounder of its customs, the arbiter of its manners. He is listened to with deference, he is addressed with respect, and the love which is felt for him is always tempered with fear.

When the condition of society becomes democratic, and men adopt as their general principle that it is good and lawful to judge of all things for oneself, using former points of belief not as a rule of faith but simply as a means of information, the power which the opinions of a father exercise over those of his sons diminishes as well as his legal power.

Perhaps the subdivision of estates which democracy brings with it contributes more than anything else to change the relations existing between a father and his children. When the property of the father of a family is scanty, his son and himself constantly live in the same place, and share the same occupations: habit and necessity bring them together, and force them to hold constant communication: the inevitable consequence is a sort of familiar intimacy, which renders authority less absolute, and which can ill be reconciled with the external forms of respect.

Now in democratic countries the class of those who are possessed of small fortunes is precisely that which gives strength to the notions, and particular direction to the manners, of the community. That class makes its opinions preponderate as universally as its will, and even those who are most inclined to resist its commands are carried away in the end by its example. I have known eager opponents of democracy who allowed their children to address them with perfect colloquial equality.

Thus, at the same time that the power of aristocracy is declining, the austere, the conventional, and the legal part of parental authority vanishes, and a species of equality prevails around the domestic hearth. I know not, upon the whole, whether society loses by the change, but I am inclined to believe that man individually is a gainer by it. I think that, in proportion as manners and laws become more democratic, the relation of father and son becomes more intimate and more affectionate; rules and authority are less talked of; confidence and tenderness are oftentimes increased, and it would seem that the natural bond is drawn closer in proportion as the social bond is loosened.

In a democratic family the father exercises no other power than that with which men love to invest the affection and the experience of age; his orders would perhaps be disobeyed, but his advice is for the most part authoritative. Though he be not hedged in with ceremonial respect, his sons at least accost him with confidence; no settled form of speech is appropriated to the mode of addressing him, but they speak to him constantly, and are ready to consult him day by day: the master and the constituted ruler have vanished,—the father remains.

Nothing more is needed, in order to judge of the difference between the two states of society in this respect, than to peruse the family correspondence of aristocratic ages. The style is always correct, ceremonious, stiff, and so cold that the natural warmth of the heart can hardly be felt in the language. The language on the contrary addressed by a son to his father in democratic countries is always marked by mingled freedom, familiarity and affection, which at once show that new relations have sprung up in the bosom of the family.

A similar revolution takes place in the mutual relations of children. In aristocratic families, as well as in aristocratic society, every place is marked out beforehand. Not only does the father occupy a separate rank, in which he enjoys extensive privileges, but even the children are not equal amongst themselves. The age and sex of each irrevocably determine his rank, and secure to him certain privileges: most of these distinctions are abolished or diminished by democracy.

In aristocratic families the eldest son, inheriting the greater part of the property, and almost all the rights of the family, becomes the chief, and to a certain extent, the master, of his brothers. Greatness and power are for him,—for them, mediocrity and dependence. Nevertheless it would be wrong to suppose that, amongst aristocratic nations, the privileges of the eldest son are advantageous to himself alone, or that they excite nothing but envy and hatred in those around him. The eldest son commonly endeavours to procure wealth and power for his brothers, because the general splendour of the house is reflected back on him who represents it; the younger sons seek to back the elder brother in all his undertakings, because the greatness and power of the head of the family better enable him to provide for all its branches. The different members of an aristocratic family are therefore very closely bound together; their interests are connected, their minds agree, but their hearts are seldom in harmony.

Democracy also binds brothers to each other, but by very different means. Under democratic laws all the children are perfectly equal, and consequently independent: nothing brings them forcibly together, but nothing keeps them apart; and as they have the same origin, as they are trained under the same roof, as they are treated with the same care, and as no peculiar privilege distinguishes or divides them, the affectionate and youthful intimacy of early years easily springs up between them. Scarcely any opportunities occur to break the tie thus formed at the outset of life; for their brotherhood brings them daily together, without embarrassing them. It is not then by interest, but by common associations and by the free sympathy of opinion and of taste, that democracy unites brothers to each other. It divides their inheritance, but it allows their hearts and minds to mingle together.

Such is the charm of these democratic manners, that even the partisans of aristocracy are caught by it; and after having experienced it for some time, they are by no means tempted to revert to the respectful and frigid observances of aristocratic families. They would be glad to retain the domestic habits of democracy, if they might throw off its social conditions and its laws; but these elements are indissolubly united, and it is impossible to enjoy the former without enduring the latter.

The remarks I have made on filial love and fraternal affection are applicable to all the passions which emanate spontaneously from human nature itself.

If a certain mode of thought or feeling is the result of some peculiar condition of life, when that condition is altered nothing whatever remains of the thought or feeling. Thus a law may bind two members of the community very closely to one another; but that law being abolished, they stand asunder. Nothing was more strict than the tie which united the vassal to the lord under the feudal system: at the present day the two men know not each other: the fear, the gratitude, and the affection which formerly connected them have vanished, and not a vestige of the tie remains.

Such, however, is not the case with those feelings which are natural to mankind. Whenever a law attempts to tutor these feelings in any particular manner, it seldom fails to weaken them; by attempting to add to their intensity, it robs them of some of their elements, for they are never stronger than when left to themselves.

Democracy, which destroys or obscures almost all the old conventional rules of society, and which prevents men from readily assenting to new ones, entirely effaces most of the feelings to which these conventional rules have given rise; but it only modifies some others, and frequently imparts to them a degree of energy and sweetness unknown before.

Perhaps it is not impossible to condense into a single proposition the whole meaning of this chapter, and of several others that preceded it. Democracy loosens social ties, but it draws the ties of nature more tight; it brings kindred more closely together, whilst it places the various members of the community more widely apart. . . .

I have shown how democracy destroys or modifies the different inequalities which originate in society: but is this all? or does it not ultimately affect that great inequality of man and woman which has seemed, up to the present day, to be eternally based in human nature? I believe that the social changes which bring nearer to the same level the father and son, the master and servant, and superiors and inferiors generally speaking, will raise woman and make her more and more the equal of man. But here, more than ever, I feel the necessity of making myself clearly understood; for there is no subject on which the coarse and lawless fancies of our age have taken a freer range.

There are people in Europe who, confounding together the different characteristics of the sexes, would make of man and woman beings not only equal but alike. They would give to both the same functions, impose on both the same duties, and grant to both the same rights; they would mix them in all things,—their occupations, their pleasures, their business. It may readily be conceived, that by thus attempting to make one sex equal to the other, both are degraded; and from so preposterous a medley of the words of nature, nothing could ever result but weak men and disorderly women.

It is not thus that the Americans understand that species of democratic equality which may be established between the sexes. They admit, that as nature has appointed such wide differences between the physical and moral constitution of man and woman, her manifest design was to give a distinct employment to their various faculties; and they hold that improvement does not consist in making beings so dissimilar do pretty nearly the same things, but in getting each of them to fulfil their respective tasks in the best possible manner. The Americans have applied to the sexes the great principle of political economy which governs the manufactures of our age, by carefully dividing the duties of man from those of woman, in order that the great work of society may be the better carried on.

In no country has such constant care been taken as in America to trace two clearly distinct lines of action for the two sexes, and to make them keep pace one with the other, but in two pathways which are always different. American women never manage the outward concerns of the family, or conduct a business, or take a part in political life; nor are they, on the other hand, ever compelled to perform the rough labour of the fields, or to make any of those laborious exertions which demand the exertion of physical strength. No families are so poor as to form an exception to this rule. If on the one hand an American woman cannot escape from the quiet circle of domestic employments, on the other hand she is never forced to go beyond it. Hence it is that the women of America, who often exhibit a masculine strength of understanding and a manly energy, generally preserve great delicacy of personal appearance and always retain the manners of women, although they sometimes show that they have the hearts and minds of men.

Nor have the Americans ever supposed that one consequence of democratic principles is the subversion of marital power, or the confusion of the natural authorities in families. They hold that every association must have a head in order to accomplish its object, and that the natural head of the conjugal association is man. They do not therefore deny him the right of directing his partner; and they maintain, that in the smaller association of husband and wife, as well as in the great social community, the object of democracy is to regulate and legalize the powers which are necessary, not to subvert all power.

This opinion is not peculiar to one sex, and contested by the other: I never observed that the women of America consider conjugal authority as a fortunate usurpation of their rights, nor that they thought themselves degraded by submitting to it. It appeared to me, on the contrary, that they attach a sort of pride to the voluntary surrender of their own will, and make it their boast to bend themselves to the yoke, not to shake it off. Such at least is the feeling expressed by the most virtuous of their sex; the others are silent; and in the United States it is not the practice for a guilty wife to clamour for the rights of women, whilst she is trampling on her holiest duties.

It has often been remarked that in Europe a certain degree of contempt lurks even in the flattery which men lavish upon women: although a European frequently affects to be the slave of woman, it may be seen that he never sincerely thinks her his equal. In the United States men seldom compliment women, but they daily show how much they esteem them. They constantly display an entire confidence in the understanding of a wife, and a profound respect for her freedom; they have decided that her mind is just as fitted as that of a man to discover the plain truth, and her heart as firm to embrace it; and they have never sought to place her virtue, any more than his, under the shelter of prejudice, ignorance, and fear.

It would seem that in Europe, where man so easily submits to the despotic sway of women, they are nevertheless curtailed of some of the greatest qualities of the human species, and considered as seductive but imperfect beings; and (what may well provoke astonishment) women ultimately look upon themselves in the same light, and almost consider it as a privilege that they are entitled to show themselves futile, feeble, and timid. The women of America claim no such privileges.

Again, it may be said, that in our morals we have reserved strange immunities to man; so that there is, as it were, one virtue for his use, and another for the guidance of his partner; and that, according to the opinion of the public, the very same act may be punished alternately as a crime, or only as a fault. The Americans know not this iniquitous division of duties and rights; amongst them the seducer is as much dishonoured as his victim.

It is true that the Americans rarely lavish upon women those eager attentions which are commonly paid them in Europe; but their conduct to women always implies that they suppose them to be virtuous and refined; and such is the respect entertained for the moral freedom of the sex, that in the presence of a woman the most guarded language is used, lest her ear should be offended by an expression. In America a young unmarried woman may, alone and without fear, undertake a long journey.

The legislators of the United States, who have mitigated almost all the penalties of criminal law, still make rape a capital offence, and no crime is visited with more inexorable severity by public opinion. This may be accounted for; as the Americans can conceive nothing more precious than a woman's honour, and nothing which ought so much to be respected as her independence, they hold that no punishment is too severe for the man who deprives her of them against her will. In France, where the same offence is visited with far milder penalties, it is frequently difficult to get a verdict from a jury against the prisoner. Is this a consequence of contempt of decency or contempt of women? I cannot but believe that it is a contempt of one and of the other.

Thus the Americans do not think that man and woman have either the duty or the right to perform the same offices, but they show an equal regard for both their respective parts; and though their lot is different, they consider both of them as beings of equal value. They do not give to the courage of woman the same form or the same direction as to that of man; but they never doubt her courage: and if they hold that man and his partner ought not always to exercise their intellect and understanding in the same manner, they at least believe the understanding of the one to be as sound as that of the other, and her intellect to be as clear. Thus, then, whilst they have allowed the social inferiority of woman to subsist, they have done all they could to raise her morally and intellectually to the level of man; and in this respect they appear to me to have excellently understood the true principle of democratic improvement.

As for myself, I do not hesitate to avow, that, although the women of the United States are confined within the narrow circle of domestic life, and their situation is in some respects one of extreme dependence, I have nowhere seen woman occupying a loftier position; and if I were asked, now that I am drawing to the close of this work, in which I have spoken of so many important things done by the Americans, to what the singular prosperity and growing strength of that people ought mainly to be attributed, I should reply,—to the superiority of their women.

Fredrika Bremer, a Swedish novelist who came to the United States in 1848, noted the assumptions governing The Homes of the New World *(London, 1853), pp. 193-96.*

The moral idea of man and of society seems clearly understood in the United States, particularly in those northern sections that have derived their population from the original colonies. I have acquainted myself with the demands made by man and society, demands for which young America fights as for its true purpose and mission. They appear to be as follows:

Every human being must be strictly true to his own individuality—must stand alone with God, and from this innermost point of view must act alone according to his own conscientious convictions.

There is no virtue peculiar to one sex which is not also a virtue in the other. Man must in morals and conduct come up to the purity of woman. Woman must possess the means of the highest development of which her nature is capable. She must, equally with man, have the opportunity of cultivating and developing her intellect. In her labors for freedom and happiness, she must possess the same rights as man.

The honor of labor and the rewards of labor ought to be equal to all. All labor is in itself honorable and must be regarded as such.

The principle of equality must govern society.

Man must become just and good through a just and good mode of treatment. Good must call forth good.

The community must give to every one of its members the best possible chance of developing his human abilities, so that he may come into possession of his human rights. This must be done both by legislation, which removes all hindrances and impediments, and by educational institutions, which give to all the opportunity for the full development of the human faculties, until they reach the age when they are capable of caring for and determining for themselves.

The ideal of society is attained in part by the individual rising up to his own ideals, in part by mutual responsibility and by those free institutions and associations which bring men into a brotherly relation with each other.

Everything for all is the true object of society. Everyone must be able to enjoy all the good things of earth, temporal as well as spiritual, according to his own capacity for enjoyment. No one must be excluded who does not exclude himself. Everyone must receive a chance of regaining his place in society. For this reason the prison must be a second school, an institution for improving those who need it. Society must, in its many sided development, so organize itself that all may be able to attain everything.

The ideal of the man of America is purity in intention, decision in will, energy in action, simplicity and gentleness in manner and demeanor. Hence there is something tender and chivalrous in his behavior to woman which is infinitely becoming to him. In every woman he respects his own mother. In the same way the woman's ideal is independence of character, gentleness of demeanor and manner.

The American's ideal of happiness is marriage and home combined with public activity. To have a wife, his own house and home, his own little piece of land, to take care of these and to beautify them, while at the same time doing some good to the state or to the city—this seems to me to be the object of human life with most men.

In the American home the women have, in general, all the power they wish. Woman is the center and the lawgiver, and the American man loves it so. He likes his wife to have her own will at home, and loves to obey it. In the happy homes in which I lived, however, I saw the wife equally careful to guide herself by the wishes of her husband.

In 1852 Francis and Theresa Pulszky, exiled Hungarian nationalists, toured the United States. Of an aristocratic heritage, they were welcomed in prominent American homes. In their White Red Black *(3 vols., London, 1853), vol. 1, pp. 77-78, 81-83, they commented upon the family of one of their hosts, Mayor Kingsland of New York City.*

It was numerous; as families generally are in America where people marry young and where society is in the happy state that many children are considered great blessings and not great cares, as is generally the case on the continent of Europe. And this, as I often had opportunity to remark in America, is not owing only to the greater facility of getting employment, but more especially to the rational view that young men have to push their own way, and that after they have got the benefit of a good education they are not to depend on their parents for support—therefore, it is not only the son of the poor and of the little-educated families who must look forward *to make himself a man.* In all classes we meet *self-made men* who, in consequence, are independent not only in position and fortunes but likewise by their practical experience, and who, for this very reason, become fit to be self-governed citizens.

Mrs. Kingsland, a mother of nine children, is one of those who, by youthful appearance, denies the prejudice that the bloom of American ladies is but short; and I have since found so frequently mothers of large families whom I mistook for the sisters of their daughters, that I may affirm that their household cares do not wear them out. . . .

It is a common boast with American gentlemen that their ladies rule, and are more respected than anywhere else in the world. I heard this often repeated in the society of New York, and I inquired of a gentleman, who was repeating this pet phrase, in what way they ruled. "Why, they have all they like," was the reply: "They dress and go shopping and have not to care about anything; we even live in hotels to save them the trouble of housekeeping."

"I see," observed I, "you are almost as courteous as the Turks, who allow their wives every amusement in their harems. The elegantly gilded parlors of your hotels, where the ladies meet to rock away time in the easy rocking chairs, are admirable harems; but what has all this to do with *the rule* of your ladies? Even granted that you accepted their wishes as commands, still you are no pashas whose whims claim obedience from the community. You, yourselves, rule only by the active part you take in public affairs, and do you mean to say you consult your ladies about these matters?"

"Well, not exactly," answered the gentleman; "but, a lady can travel alone without danger of an insult, or unbecoming behavior; our daughters go out often and are in society without their mothers—every man is their natural protector."

"Quite as in Turkey," replied I; "no man, not even the husband, would ever dare to follow his veiled lady in the streets. All the difference, perhaps, is that the morality in the United States is more sterling than in France and Italy or in the capitals of Austria and Russia, and therefore flirtations with married ladies are unheard of."

"But in Europe," he said, "women even work in the fields and they must assist the husbands to earn a subsistence; with us, even in the factories, the girls work until they marry, but once married, the maintenance of the family is the care of the husband, and an American farmer would feel degraded if his wife or daughter should hoe the corn or break the flax."

Of course, I readily acknowledged that owing to the greater facilities of earning a livelihood, the women of the lower classes were much better off than in Europe, but I did not understand in what way the respect for the fair sex is connected with this fact. The gentleman turned to other topics; I sought information on the other side, and understood from some very intellectual ladies that their lords, *in general,* little consult the opinions of their female rulers, even as concerns their own private affairs. I learned that it occurs but too often that a lady who believes herself to be in affluent circumstances is suddenly informed by her husband that they must give up housekeeping because they cannot afford it. It appears as if the gentlemen would atone for their all-absorbing passion for business by the privilege they give to the ladies of idling time away. And as business is a passion with the Americans, not the means, but the very life of existence, they are most anxious to keep this department exclusively to themselves; and, well aware that there is no more infallible way to secure noninterference, than by giving the general impression that they never act for themselves, *the lady's rule* has become a current phrase, but by no means a fact in the United States.

The nurseries are by no means the only realm of the children. They roam about the house, upstairs and down, circulating freely like little birds not confined to cages, but fluttering about the whole precinct of an ample hothouse. And thus the little ones are not abandoned to the nurses, but the mother has them constantly under her eye, though I cannot say under her control, for they have their own way. They run in and out and play, tumbling and dragging about books and cushions and chairs and climbing up and down just as they please. In consequence they never are embarrassed, and meet everyone who chances to come with the most perfect ease. Unconstrained and not preoccupied by any conventional rule, they grow strikingly sharp and answer every inquiry with a self-dependence and self-observation which never can be obtained by a training to accepted notions and habitual manners. But on the other side, such children, unaccustomed to check and to control their impulses easily become spoiled to all discipline, and this explains in a great measure the habit prevalent in America of placing even the girls at school, thus depriving the mother of her most precious privilege, the education of her own daughter.

Foreigners often made the connection between the unique authority structure within the American home and the busy, frantic pace of American life—the need to succeed in the highly competitive New

World. Some astute observations were made by Joseph Alexander Hübner, an Austrian diplomat who visited the United States in 1871. The following comments evoked by experiences in the Chicago area were taken from Baron von Hübner's Ramble Round the World, 1871, translated by Lady Herbert (New York, 1874), pp. 54-58.

In the West the towns are quickly seen, and are all alike. One may say the same of the hotels which play so great a part here, not only in the life of travelers, but in those of the residents. A great number of families, especially newly married couples, live in hotels. This method saves expenses and the bother of housekeeping; it also makes easy the frequent moves from one town to another. But it has the inconvenience of condemning the young wife to a life of idleness and solitude. All day long the husband is at his office. He comes in only at mealtimes, and then devours his food with the silence and dispatch of a starving man. Then he rushes back to his treadmill.

The children are sent to school when they are five or six years old. They go by themselves, and pass the rest of their day exactly as they please, no one thinking it right to interfere with their liberty. Paternal authority is nil, or at any rate is never exercised. There is no education in our sense of the word; but there is instruction, public, good, and accessible to all. The little gentlemen talk loudly, and are as proud and sharp as the full-grown men of their nation. The young girls at eight and nine years old excel in the arts of coquetry and flirtation, and promise to become "fast" young ladies; but nevertheless they make good and faithful wives. If their husband should be rich, they will help him ruin himself by extravagance in dress; yet they will accept misery calmly, and the moment there is a change in the wheel of fortune fly into the same follies as of old.

The home of the English, so dear to their hearts, is only a secondary consideration in the lives of their cousins beyond the seas. This is easily explained. In the New World man is born to conquer. Life is a perpetual struggle, a rivalry from which no one can exempt himself, a race in the open field across terrible obstacles, with the prospect of enormous rewards for reaching the goal. The American cannot keep his arms folded. He must embark on something, and once embarked he must go on and on forever; for if he stops, those who follow him would crush him under their feet. His life is one long campaign, a succession of never-ending fights, marches, and countermarches. In such a militant existence, what place is left for the sweetness, the repose, the intimacy of home or its joys? Is he happy? Judging by his tired, sad, exhausted, anxious, and often delicate and unhealthy appearance, one would be inclined to doubt it. Such an excess of uninterrupted labor cannot be good for any man.

The woman suffers most from this regime. She sees her husband at most for half an hour once in the day, and then in the evening, when, worn out with fatigue, he comes home to sleep. She cannot lighten his burden or share his anxiety and cares, for she knows nothing of his business; for want of time, there is little or no interchange of thought between them. As a mother, her share in the education of her children is of the smallest. As soon as her little ones can run alone they pass their lives away from her, out of the house. They are entirely ignorant of the obedience or respect due their parents but, on the other hand, learn early to do without care or protection, to be self-sufficient. They ripen quickly, and prepare themselves from their tenderest years for the fatigues and struggles of the overexciting, harsh, adventurous life which awaits them.

Besides all this, a woman boarding at one of these huge caravan-series has not even the resources and occupation which ordinary domestic details involve. Is it as a compensation for these privations that American society surrounds her with privileges and attentions unknown in the Old World? Everywhere she is the object of a respectful gallantry, which might be called chivalric were it less frivolous, and sometimes even grotesque and ridiculous. For example, I am sitting in one of these tram cars which cross all the principal streets of the great towns. A tap of a parasol or a fan rouses me from my meditations. I see standing right in front of me a young woman, who looks at me from head to foot with an imperious, haughty, even angry expression. I wake up to the situation and hasten to give her my seat, which she takes at once, without deigning to thank me, even by a look or a smile. The consequence is that I am obliged to perform the rest of my journey standing in a most uncomfortable position, and to hold on by a leather strap which is fastened for that purpose along the roof of the carriage.

On the other hand, it is the fashion to disparage American women. People call them frivolous, flirtatious, extravagant, and say that they are always running after pleasure. These accusations seem to me unjust. The American woman bears the stamp of her position and of the atmosphere around her. As a young girl she naturally follows the inclinations of her sex which are not, as with us, regulated and controlled by the teaching and example of a mother. She wishes to please, and if she is naturally lively she will become "fast"; that is, she will laugh loudly and by smart repartee and piquant looks will endeavor to attract the greatest possible number of young men. But this vulgar coquetry, however jarring to good taste, rarely goes beyond a certain point. There is always a father, a brother, or an uncle near by, armed with revolver or bowie knife, who is quite ready to ask you, with every imaginable politeness, if your intentions be fair and honorable.

Married women in America are, as a rule, unexceptionable. If they are too fond of dress, it is generally their husbands who wish it. If they are often seen abroad, it is because they have nothing to do at home. If they are rather free and easy, such manners are allowed in society; it is, after all, bad taste—not sin. Their minds are generally well cultivated, for they read a great deal, mostly novels, but also English classic authors and encyclopedias. And they attend the public lectures and literary conversations held in all the great towns of the Union.

Information concerning the effects of American social values on the home was especially welcomed by Europeans who were considering emigration. A working-class Scotsman, James D. Burn, who visited the United States from 1862 to 1865, warned his fellow countrymen what to expect if they went to the New World. In Three Years among the Working Classes in the United States *(London, 1865), pp. 77-78, 86-87, 91-93, he wrote:*

The principle of equality laid down in the Constitution of the United States has influenced in a remarkable manner the condition of the women of the country. It may be that the world has heretofore been wrong in according to man a mental and physical superiority over woman, and that until the latter end of the Eighteenth Century, he usurped a controlling power in society to which he had no right.

Whether this be so or not, the American women have taken what they deem their proper position in society, and according to their own manner of expressing themselves, if they cannot boss it over the men they will not be bossed, which simply means if they cannot be masters they will not be mastered. A married woman in the ranks of the working-classes in England knows she has certain household duties to perform, and she does them with order and regularity. She has learned to look up to her husband, not as a master, but as a lover and protector. She has two strong motives for studying his health and attending to his wants and wishes—her affection is the first, and her self-interest the second. From the general nature of domestic arrangements the man and his wife slide as it were into their respective duties; he works for the siller, and she lays it out to the best advantage, and makes him a home in the best sense of the term.

In all civilized society, if we except America, women, from the very nature of their weakness, look up to man as a power above them, but they esteem that power with feelings of love rather than fear. In America, female notions of equality and personal independence have to a great extent reversed the old order of things in the relation of the sexes to each other. Among the class of married people who keep house it is a common thing for the man to do a considerable part of the slip-slop work. In the morning he lights the stove-fire, empties the slops, makes ready his own breakfast, and if his work lies at a distance he packs up his midday meal, and leaving his wife in bed, he packs himself off to his work. Even among the trading classes who have private dwellings, it is quite common to see the men bringing parcels from the market, the grocer's, fishmonger's, or butcher's, for the morning meal. It may be supposed from this bending of masculine dignity in the dishclout-service of their wives, the men are examples of kind and affectionate husbands, and that the ladies are so many connubial doves! But this would be a hasty conclusion. Since the opening of the Divorce Court in England strange disclosures have been made of the mystery of married life, and civilized humanity has often been startled by the savage conduct of its members. But though selfishness, incompatibility of temper, and even brutality of disposition have caused much suffering, the bond of matrimony as it exists in the old country is esteemed not the less a holy tie and a safeguard of public morality. In America, notwithstanding the ready performance of the domestic duties mentioned above, the matrimonial tie is comparatively loose. The woman who has made up her mind not to be bossed by her husband, which means that she will do as she likes irrespective of his will, is not likely to run smoothly in hymeneal harness, and this is the case with a large number of wives in the lower stratum of society. But here again a distinction must be drawn between the natives and the immigrants. I have reason to believe that the real American women make by far the best wives and mothers. . . .

I certainly would not advise a working-man with a young family to bring them out here, particularly if he intend to settle in a town. As I have already said, children, after having been in this country a short time, learn to throw off the restraints of parental authority; they are soon made to feel that they are in a land of liberty, and long before they arrive at the age of mature judgment, they are members of the sovereign people, and therefore conceive themselves equal to anybody and everybody. I do not know any task more difficult than for a father in this country to keep his children well in hand. Whether they go to school or pick up their education among their playmates, they are almost certain to imbibe notions of personal independence at an early stage subversive of all home authority. Self-reliance is no doubt a very desirable thing when not inconsistent with filial love and duty, but without these virtues it becomes a thing of mere pride and selfishness. I have heard the members of a family tell their parents that they were under no obligation to them, either for bringing them into the world or rearing them. Though this heartless doctrine may not always find expression in words, I believe it is but too frequently acted upon by young America.

The gallantry of the American men, the purity of sentiment, the refinement of manners and the amiable politeness of her women, have long been held up to the rest of the civilized world as moral and social traits of character to be admired rather than imitated. So long as women are in a decided minority, it is only natural that men should pet and flatter them, and it is not wonderful that the deference then paid should be claimed by the darlings themselves as a prescriptive right. How far this constrained gallantry of the men, and the purity and politeness of the women, are really in advance of Old World morality, is another question, and becomes extremely doubtful when the ruderess with which women are treated in private is considered.

If the gentlemen's gallantry were the result of good breeding, they would certainly avoid the use of profane language, expectorating regardless of time or place, and elevating their understandings in the presence of the ladies. These masculine habits, however, may be matters which foreigners do not understand in the every-day life of a people whose civilization is based upon human equality and social freedom. . . .

Go-aheadism is as common among many of the women in the United States as it is in the ranks of the men. When at home, it is quite a common practice to come and go without asking leave or taking counsel. Matrimony in the old country is looked upon as a bond of union effected by mutual affection; but from what I have witnessed, a goodly number of both sexes here possess very different ideas upon the subject. The philosophy of "adaptability" regulates the conduct of not a few married people who have promised to love, honour, and obey. In the first blush of married life many of the young men and women mistake passion for that deep-seated feeling which should unite two sympathies in one; and when they find that they do not run smoothly together in matrimonial traces, one or the other flies off. These *halves* of disappointed beings are to be met in every direction, and if one of these ladies should have the misfortune to become a mother, ten to one but she will relieve herself of the responsibility by transferring her child to a stranger for adoption. Women do not wear the charms of youth long under the changing temperature of America; they are aware of the melancholy fact, and as a consequence the fast ladies make up their minds to enjoy life as best they may, and so long as their feelings are warmed by the fire of youth.

Within the range of my own experience I have known several second-hand wives who were sailing under the black flags of widowhood, and fishing for other experimental partners. The peculiar notions of personal independence indulged in by the women's rights' ladies in America, has been the means of placing a great portion of the fabric of female society in a false position. Woman was evidently designed to be the companion of man, and as he is stronger, both mentally and physically, it follows as a necessary consequence that he is a power above her; this power, however, when properly exercised, is directed to shield her from harm as well as be a means for her support. The class of ladies I refer to take a different view of the matter; they are not content to hold the position Providence has placed them in as handmaidens to the men, but they too must be rulers beyond the regions of the kitchen and nursery. In thus speaking of the American ladies, I allude to that large class whose notions of equality lead them to be more than the equals of their husbands. If a man marries a woman who has been employed at any of the sedentary avocations, and cannot place her in a house of his own fitted up to her taste, she will prefer to take up her residence in a boarding establishment, where she can have a good table and enjoy the luxury of idleness, and have both time and opportunity for flirtation. I was in the company of a woman a short time ago who had left her husband because, among other things, he did not allow her more than thirteen dollars a week, out of which she had to provide food for themselves and a baby; the husband paying rent, coals, and clothing. This model wife was the partner of a sober, hard-working man. The father has the child, and she is performing in the character of a young widow in a boardinghouse in another State, two hundred miles from all her woman's heart should hold dear.

Toward the end of the nineteenth century, foreign observers ceased referring to the abstract ideal of equality as an explanation of the uniqueness of the American woman. Increasingly they suggested that education and social roles made the American female different from her European counterpart. James F. Muirhead, the English editor of Baedeker's guide to the United States, pursued this line of reasoning in The Land of Contrasts *(originally published in 1898; London, 1900 ed.), pp. 46-51.*

The European visitor to the United States *has* to write about American women because they bulk so largely in his view, because they seem essentially so prominent a feature of American life, because their *relative* importance and interest impress him as greater than those of women in the lands of the Old World, because they seem to him to embody in so eminent a measure that intangible quality of Americanism, the existence, or indeed the possibility, of which is so hotly denied by some Americans.

Indeed, those who look upon the prominent rôle of the American woman merely as one phase of the "new woman" question—merely as the inevitable conspicuousness of woman intruding on what has hitherto been exclusively the sphere of man—are many degrees beside the point. The American note is as obvious in the girl who has never taken the slightest interest in politics, the professions, or even the bicycle. . . .

It seems a reasonable assumption that the formation of the American girl is due to the same large elemental causes that account for American phenomena generally; and her *relative* strikingness may be explained by the reflection that there was more room for these great forces to work in the case of woman than in the case of man. The Englishman, for instance, through his contact with public life and affairs, through his wider experience, through his rubbing shoulders with more varied types, had already been prepared for the working of American conditions in a way that his more sheltered womankind had not been. In the bleaching of the black and the grey, the change will be the more striking in the former; the recovery of health will be conspicuous in proportion to the gravity of the disease. America has meant opportunity for women even more in some ways than for men. The gap between them has been lessened in proportion as the gap between the American and the European has widened. The average American woman is distinctly more different from her average English sister than is the case with their respective brothers. The training of the English girl starts from the very beginning on a different basis from that of the boy; she is taught to restrain her impulses, while his are allowed much freer scope; the sister is expected to defer to the brother from the time she can walk or talk. In America this difference of training is constantly tending to the vanishing point. The American woman has never learned to play second fiddle. The American girl, as Mr. Henry James says, is rarely negative; she is either (and usually) a most charming success or (and exceptionally) a most disastrous failure. The pathetic army of ineffective spinsters clinging apologetically to the skirts of gentility is conspicuous by its absence in America. The conditions of life there encourage a girl to undertake what she can do best, with a comparatively healthy disregard of its fancies "respectability." Her consciousness of efficiency reacts in a thousand ways; her feet are planted on so solid a foundation that she inevitably seems an important constructive part of society. . . .

The American woman, too, has had more time than the American man to cultivate the more amiable—if you will, the more showy—qualities of American civilisation. The leisured class of England consists of both sexes, that of America pratically of one only. The problem of the American man so far has mainly been to subdue a new continent to human uses, while the woman has been sacrificing on the altar of the Graces. Hence the wider culture and the more liberal views are often found in the sex from which the European does not expect them; hence the woman of New York and other American cities is often conspicuously superior to her husband in looks, manners, and general intelligence. This has been denied by champions of the American man; but the observation of the writer, whatever it may be worth, would deny the denial.

Put roughly, what chiefly strikes the stranger in the American woman is her candour, her frankness, her hail-fellow-well-met-edness, her apparent absence of consciousness of self or of sex, her spontaneity, her vivacity, her fearlessness. If the observer himself is not of a specially refined or delicate type, he is apt at first to misunderstand the cameraderie of an American girl, to see in it suggestions of a possible coarseness of fibre. If a vain man, he may take it as a tribute to his personal charms, or at least to the superior claims of a representative of old-world civilisation. But even to the obtuse stranger of this character it will ultimately become obvious—as to the more refined observer *ab initio*—that he can no more (if as much) dare to take a liberty with the American girl than with his own countrywoman. The plum may appear to be more easily handled, but its bloom will be found to be as intact and as ethereal as in the jealously guarded hothouse fruit of Europe. He will find that her frank and charming companionability is as far removed from masculinity as from coarseness; that the points in which she differs from the European lady do not bring her nearer either to a man on the one hand, or to a common woman on the other. He will find that he has to readjust his standards, to see that divergence from the best type of woman hitherto known to him does not necessarily mean deterioration; if he is of an open and susceptible mind, he may even come to the conclusion that he prefers the transatlantic type!

Muirhead also commented on the American child (The Land of Contrasts, *pp. 63-64, 70-71*).

The United States has sometimes been called the "Paradise of Women;" from the child's point of view it might equally well be termed the "Paradise of Children," though the thoughtful observer might be inclined to qualify the title by the prefix "Fools." Nowhere is the child so constantly in evidence; nowhere are his wishes so carefully consulted; nowhere is he allowed to make his mark so strongly on society in general. The difference begins at the very moment of his birth, or indeed even sooner. As much fuss is made over each young republican as if he were the heir to a long line of kings; his swaddling clothes might make a ducal infant jealous; the family physician thinks $100 or $150 a moderate fee for ushering him into the light of day. Ordinary milk is not good enough for him; *sterilised* milk will hardly do; *"modified"* milk alone is considered fit for this democratic suckling. Even the father is expected to spend hours in patient consultation over his food, his dress, his teething-rings, and his outgoing. He is weighed daily, and his nourishment is changed at once if he is a fraction either behind or ahead of what is deemed a normal and healthy rate of growth. American writers on the care of children give directions for the use of the most complex and time-devouring devices for the proper preparation of their food, and seem really to expect that mamma and nurse will go through with the prescribed juggling with pots and pans, cylinders and lamps.

A little later the importance of the American child is just as evident, though it takes on different forms. The small American seems to consider himself the father of the man in a way never contemplated by the poet. He interrupts the conversation of his elders, he has a voice in every matter, he eats and drinks what seems good to him, he (or at any rate *she*) wears finger-rings of price, he has no shyness or even modesty. The theory of the equality of man is rampant in the nursery (though I use this word only in its conventional and figurative sense, for American children do not confine themselves to their nurseries). You will actually hear an American mother say of a child of two or three years of age: "I can't *induce* him to do this;" "She *won't* go to bed when I tell her;" "She *will* eat that lemon pie, though I *know* it is bad for her". . . .

The strangest thing about the matter is, however, that the fruit does not by any means correspond to the seed; the wind is sown, but the whirlwind is not reaped. The unendurable child does not necessarily become an intolerable man. By some mysterious chemistry of the American atmosphere, social or otherwise, the horrid little minx blossoms out into a charming and womanly girl, with just enough of independence to make her piquant; the cross and dyspeptic little boy becomes a courteous and amiable man. Some sort of a moral miracle seems to take place about the age of fourteen or fifteen; a violent dislocation interrupts the natural continuity of progress; and, presto! out springs a new creature from the modern cauldron of Medea.

The reason—or at any rate one reason—of the normal attitude of the American parent towards his child is not far to seek. It is almost undoubtedly one of the direct consequences of the circumambient spirit of democracy. The American is so accustomed to recognise the essential equality of others that he sometimes carries a good thing to excess. This spirit is seen in his dealings with underlings of all kinds, who are rarely addressed with the bluntness and brusqueness of the older civilisations. Hence the father and mother are apt to lay almost too much stress on the separate and individual entity of the child, to shun too scrupulously anything approaching the violent coercion of another's will. That the results are not more disastrous seems owing to a saving quality in the child himself. The characteristic American shrewdness and common sense do their work. A badly brought up American child introduced into a really well-regulated family soon takes his cue from his surroundings, adapts himself to his new conditions, and sheds his faults as a snake its skin. The whole process may tend to increase the individuality of the child; but the cost is often great, the consequences hard for the child itself. American parents are doubtless more familiar than others with the plaintive remonstrance: "Why did you not bring me up more strictly? Why did you give me so much of my own way?" The present type of the American child may be described as one of the experiments of democracy; that he is not a necessary type is proved by the by no means insignificant number of excellently trained children in the United States, of whom it has never been asserted that they make any less truly democratic citizens than their more pampered playmates.

An alternative explanation for the character of the American child was the American sense of liberty, an insistence by the parents themselves that their children become independent. Paul de Rousiers, a Frenchman who visited the United States in 1891, suggested this idea in his American Life, *trans. A. J. Herbertson (New York, 1892), pp. 254-58.*

An American, five years old, is already very different from a European, as can be seen in a thousand details. Last year, when I was returning from New York to Havre, there were several American families on the steamer. The children, who are usually free from seasickness, were one of the greatest sources of interest to me during the voyage. Their ways and talk, which I compared with the ways and the talk of French children, were most instructive and sometimes threw a vivid light on all that I had seen in America. One day, when I was marching up and down the hundred yards of deck, I saw a little girl about four years old climb on the railing and lean half over right above the water. I instinctively drew nearer to save her should she fall, when her mother, happening to pass, said to her, "Well, are you having a good time?" patted her on the cheek, and then went off to the other end of the vessel to play at skipping ropes with two or three gentlemen who had got up that little game to relieve the tedium of the voyage. I then resumed my interrupted walk, saying to myself that there was no need to be more motherly than a mother, and thinking about my wife and children. What fears a French mother would have had in like circumstances! This American mother was by no means an unnatural one; far from it. She considered some things to be natural and salutary which we think foolish and imprudent. Her code is that each one should be able to look after himself, and she naturally applies it to her child, not because she has reasoned the matter out, but because it is customary, and she has no idea that her action could raise the slightest whisper of criticism.

There are doubtless many objections to this way of doing things which are obvious enough, but the American accepts these, believing that they are not so important as the advantages; their children are imprudent, but their youths are bold and enterprising. We, on the other hand, wish our children to be quiet, obedient, under control, and our young people lack initiative. From the care of a nurse they pass to that of a servant, from that of a school-usher to that of a mess corporal, and when they are given their freedom, they do not know what to do with it. . . .

In a word, the Americans accustom their children to look after themselves from an early age, to have confidence in themselves and to need nobody. When traveling one can see little girls of seven or eight, packing their trunks themselves; each has her own and is responsible for it; she orders what she wants at meal-time and knows how to choose. A well-bred child in our country looks at her mother to see if she may accept a bit of candy.

They are early taught that life has its painful necessities, and that it is useless to bewail the departure of their father on a long journey, or the reverses of fortune. They are virilely educated.

American parents do not usually do these things from any special reasoning, any more than French parents have a special theory about the education they give their children; but the tyrany of custom brings it about.

Further, an American father and mother preach mainly by example; they do not often correct their children and they seldom use force. The reason will be found in that which I have said before—to develop initiative it is necessary to let alone. Hence extraordinary patience and requests where we would command. In a village in the West a young mother said before me to her little girl of three years, who had been making a mess in the parlor, "Arabella, please do not do that. I am very sorry, but I must forbid you to do that. Arabella, you will break my heart." That woman's heart would be in many pieces before evening, for Arabella broke it every instant. I have heard many tales like this. A little boy, who had been expelled from several schools in St. Paul, returned home after one of these escapades. The father, without disturbing himself, said, "Well, sir, what college do you intend to go to now?" It is impossible to stretch respect for individual liberty farther.

It often happens that a ten-year-old American plays the part of a little man, as is inevitable with such liberty as he has; but the manifestations of his precocity are serious in spite of their ridiculousness. He does not think himself a man because he smokes, walks with his toes turned out, or speaks of popular actresses. What raises him in his own eyes is to have some responsibility, or to give himself the air of having it; for instance, to look after his little sister and conduct her to his father's carriage. Above all, he affects absolute independence, and talks of the business he is going to do, about which he is already thinking.

However, in spite of this almost negative education I have just described, in spite of the great liberty which the young American is allowed in everything, there is one exception to this liberty which is carefully taken from him—the liberty of *doing nothing* in the future. The feeling of responsibility is developed to prepare him to be perfectly responsible for the means of his existence as soon as he is old enough. If a youth even of sixteen or seventeen, or of twenty at the oldest, has to ask his father to help him with money, his comrades point their fingers at him. Public opinion is strong on this point, and the fathers of families do not intend to feed the strapping fellows they have brought up; and so the beardless youth has to shift for himself, and it is for him to prove that he has stuff in him and can manage his own affairs.

III. RELIGION AND PUBLIC MORALITY

Foreign visitors agreed that the religious principles and zeal of the Americans permeated their political institutions and supported their social attitudes. Yet Church and State were separate in the United States, unlike the situation in Europe. How did European observers explain the fact that whereas the religious and political spheres were separate by law, religion was nevertheless interwoven in the entire fabric of American life even more than it was in Europe? How did they relate the spirit of religion to the spirit of freedom in the United States? Why did they consider religion essential to the American Constitution? How important was religion as an element in public opinion? What difficulties faced American clergymen?

In Democracy in America, *trans. Henry Reeve (London, 1862), vol. 1, pp. 365-70, Alexis de Tocqueville explained the principal causes of the importance of religion in the United States.*

The philosophers of the eighteenth century explained the gradual decay of religious faith in a very simple manner. Religious zeal, said they, must necessarily fail, the more generally liberty is established and knowledge diffused. Unfortunately, facts are by no means in accordance with their theory. There are certain populations in Europe whose unbelief is only equalled by their ignorance and their debasement, whilst in America one of the freest and most enlightened nations in the world fulfils all the outward duties of religion with fervour.

Upon my arrival in the United States, the religious aspect of the country was the first thing that struck my attention; and the longer I stayed there, the more did I perceive the great political consequences resulting from this state of things, to which I was unaccustomed. In France I had almost always seen the spirit of religion and the spirit of freedom pursuing courses diametrically opposed to each other; but in America I found that they were intimately united, and that they reigned in common over the same country. My desire to discover the causes of this phenomenon increased from day to day. In order to satisfy it, I questioned the members of all the different sects: and I more especially sought the society of the clergy, who are the depositaries of the different persuasions, and who are more especially interested in their duration. As a member of the Roman Catholic Church I was more particularly brought into contact with several of its priests, with whom I became intimately acquainted. To each of these men I expressed my astonishment and I explained my doubts: I found that they differed upon matters of detail alone; and that they mainly attributed the peaceful dominion of religion in their country, to the separation of Church and State. I do not hesitate to affirm that during my stay in America, I did not meet with a single individual, of the clergy or of the laity, who was not of the same opinion upon this point.

This led me to examine more attentively than I had hitherto done, the station which the American clergy occupy in political society. I learned with surprise that they filled no public appointments; not one of them is to be met with in the administration, and they are not even represented in the legislative assemblies. In several States the law excludes them from political life; public opinion in all. And when I came to inquire into the prevailing spirit of the clergy, I found that most of its members seemed to retire of their own accord from the exercise of power, and that they made it the pride of their profession to abstain from politics.

I heard them inveigh against ambition and deceit, under whatever political opinions these vices might chance to lurk; but I learned from their discourses that men are not guilty in the eye of God for any opinions concerning political government, which they may profess with sincerity, any more than they are for their mistakes in building a house or in driving a furrow. I perceived that these ministers of the Gospel eschewed all parties, with the anxiety attendant upon personal interest. These facts convinced me that what I had been told was true; and it then became my object to investigate their causes, and to inquire how it happened that the real authority of religion was increased by a state of things which diminished its apparent force: these causes did not long escape my researches.

The short space of threescore years can never content the imagination of man; nor can the imperfect joys of this world satisfy his heart. Man alone, of all created beings, displays a natural contempt of existence, and yet a boundless desire to exist; he scorns life, but he dreads annihilation. These different feelings incessantly urge his soul to the contemplation of a future state, and religion directs his musings thither. Religion, then, is simply another form of hope; and it is no less natural to the human heart than hope itself. Men cannot abandon their religious faith without a kind of aberration of intellect, and a sort of violent distortion of their true natures; but they are invincibly brought back to more pious sentiments; for unbelief is an accident, and faith is the only permanent state of mankind. If we only consider religious institutions in a purely human point of view, they may be said to derive an inexhaustible element of strength from man himself, since they belong to one of the constituent principles of human nature.

I am aware that at certain times, religion may strengthen this influence, which originates in itself, by the artificial power of the laws, and by the support of those temporal institutions which direct society. Religions, intimately united to the governments of the earth, have been known to exercise a sovereign authority derived from the twofold source of terror and of faith; but when a religion contracts an alliance of this nature, I do not hesitate to affirm that it commits the same error, as a man who should sacrifice his future to his present welfare; and in obtaining a power to which it has no claim, it risks that authority which is rightfully its own. When a religion founds its empire upon the desire of immortality which lives in every human heart, it may aspire to universal dominion; but when it connects itself with a government, it must necessarily adopt maxims which are only applicable to certain nations. Thus, in forming an alliance with a political power, religion augments its authority over a few, and forfeits the hope of reigning over all.

As long as a religion rests upon those sentiments which are the consolation of all affliction, it may attract the affections of mankind. But if it be mixed up with the bitter passions of the world, it may be constrained to defend allies whom its interests, and not the principle of love, have given to it; or to repel as antagonists men who are still attached to its own spirit, however opposed they may be to the powers to which it is allied. The Church cannot share the temporal power of the State, without being the object of a portion of that animosity which the latter excites.

The political powers which seem to be most firmly established have frequently no better guarantee for their duration, than the opinions of a generation, the interests of the time, or the life of an individual. A law may modify the social condition which seems to be most fixed and determinate; and with the social condition everything else must change. The powers of society are more or less fugitive, like the years which we spend upon the earth; they succeed each other with rapidity like the fleeting cares of life; and no government has ever yet been founded upon an invariable disposition of the human heart, or upon an imperishable interest.

As long as a religion is sustained by those feelings, propensities, and passions which are found to occur under the same forms, at all the different periods of history, it may defy the efforts of time; or at least it can only be destroyed by another religion. But when religion clings to the interests of the world, it becomes almost as fragile a thing as the powers of earth. It is the only one of them all which can hope for immortality; but if it be connected with their ephemeral authority, it shares their fortunes, and may fall with those transient passions which supported them for a day. The alliance which religion contracts with political powers must needs be onerous to itself; since it does not require their assistance to live, and by giving them its assistance it may be exposed to decay.

The danger which I have just pointed out always exists, but it is not always equally visible. In some ages governments seem to be imperishable, in others the existence of society appears to be more precarious than the life of man. Some constitutions plunge the citizens into a lethargic somnolence, and others rouse them to feverish excitement. When governments appear to be so strong, and laws so stable, men do not perceive the dangers which may accrue from a union of Church and State. When governments display so much weakness, and laws so much inconstancy, the danger is self-evident, but it is no longer impossible to avoid it; to be effectual, measures must be taken to discover its approach.

In proportion as a nation assumes a democratic condition of society, and as communities display democratic propensities, it becomes more and more dangerous to connect religion with political institutions; for the time is coming when authority will be bandied from hand to hand, when political theories will succeed each other, and when men, laws, and constitutions will disappear or be modified from day to day, and this, not for a season only, but unceasingly. Agitation and mutability are inherent in the nature of democratic republics, just as stagnation and inertness are the law of absolute monarchies.

If the Americans, who change the head of the Government once in four years, who elect new legislators every two years, and renew the provincial officers every twelve-month; if the Americans, who have abandoned the political world to the attempts of innovators, had not placed religion beyond their reach, where could it abide in the ebb and flow of human opinions? where would that respect which belongs to it be paid, amidst the struggles of faction? and what would become of its immortality, in the midst of perpetual decay? The American clergy were the first to perceive this truth, and to act in conformity with it. They saw that they must renounce their religious influence, if they were to strive for political power; and they chose to give up the support of the State, rather than to share its vicissitudes.

In America, religion is perhaps less powerful than it has been at certain periods in the history of certain peoples; but its influence is more lasting. It restricts itself to its own resources, but of those none can deprive it: its circle is limited to certain principles, but those principles are entirely its own and under its undisputed control.

Born in Bohemia in 1805, Francis Grund emigrated to the United States as a young man, practiced journalism in Philadelphia, and subsequently served in the American diplomatic corps in Europe. In his two-volume work on The Americans in their Moral, Social, and Political Relations *(London, 1837), vol. 1, pp. 292-301, he explained how religion was connected not only to politics, but also to law, public morality, and public opinion.*

The religious habits of the Americans form not only the basis of their private and public morals, but have become so thoroughly interwoven with their whole course of legislation that it would be impossible to change them without affecting the very essence of their government. Not only are the manners and habits of a people, at all times, stronger than the positive law, but the latter itself is never readily obeyed without becoming reduced to a custom. It is to the manners and habits of a nation we must look for the continuance of their government. In France, where the people have for ages been accustomed to an absolute and despotic government, where every historical monument, every palace, every work of art, nay, the very furniture of their rooms, speak monarchy, we perceive constant anomalies in society, from the legislative halls down to the meanest public resort; simply because the people are accustomed to feel one way, and constrained to reason and act in another. They possess yet the forms of religion, which have ceased to convey to them a meaning; they have yet the splendor of a throne, without any of the feelings of loyalty; they have all the titles and pretensions of their ancient nobles, with the most unbounded love of equality. Yet, with all their political excitability, and their theoretical attachment to republicanism, they are constantly lulled asleep by monarchical principles without offering any other resistance than the sensation which the fact itself produces, when set off by the pen of an editor. An Englishman or an American would feel the encroachment on his liberty, because it would oblige him to change his habits, which he is less prepared to do, than to surrender a positive right. American liberty is further advanced in the minds of the people than even in the laws themselves. It has become an active principle which lives with, and animates the nation, and of which their political constitution is but a facsimile.

Whatever contributes to confirm a people in the habitual exercise of freedom is an additional guarantee of its continuance; and whatever has been instrumental in procuring that freedom, or is associated with it in their minds, must be preserved with religious care, lest liberty itself should suffer in their estimation. This is the case with the doctrines of Christianity in the United States. Religion has been the basis of the most important American settlements; religion kept their little community together; religion assisted them in their revolutionary struggle, it was religion to which they appealed in defending their rights, and it was religion, in fine, which taught them to prize their liberties. It is with the solemnities of religion that the Declaration of Independence is yet annually read to the people from the pulpit, or that Americans celebrate the anniversaries of the most important events in their history. It is to religion they have recourse whenever they wish to impress the popular feeling with anything relative to their country; and it is religion which assists them in all their national undertakings. The Americans look upon religion as a promoter of civil and political liberty; and have, therefore, transferred it to a large portion of the affection which they cherish for the institutions of their country. In other countries, where religion has become the instrument of oppression, it has been the policy of the liberal party to diminish its influence; but in America its promotion is essential to the constitution.

Religion presides over their councils, aids in the execution of the laws, and adds to the dignity of the judges. Whatever is calculated to diminish its influence and practice has a tendency to weaken the government, and is, consequently, opposed to the peace and welfare of the United States. It would have a direct tendency to lessen the respect for the law, to bring disorder into their public deliberations, and to retard the administration of justice.

The deference which the Americans pay to morality is scarcely inferior to their regard for religion, and is, in part, based upon the latter. The least solecism in the moral conduct of a man is attributed to his want of religion, and is visited upon him as such. It is not the offense itself, but the outrage on society, which is punished. They see in a breach of morals a direct violation of religion; and in this, an attempt to subvert the political institutions of the country. These sentiments are all-powerful in checking the appearance of vice, even if they are not always sufficient to preclude its existence.

With Argus-eyes does public opinion watch over the words and actions of individuals, and, whatever may be their private sins, enforces at least a tribute to morality in public.

My meaning cannot be misunderstood. It is but the open violation of the law, which comes before the forum of the judge; for our secret transgressions we shall have to account with our God. Public virtue must be guarded against the pernicious influence of example; vice must be obliged to conceal itself, in order not to tincture society in general. In this consists the true force and wholesome influence of public opinion. It becomes a mighty police-agent of morality and religion, which not only discovers crimes, but partly prevents their commission. The whole people of the United States are empanelled as a permanent jury to pronounce their verdict of "guilty" or "not guilty" on the conduct and actions of men, from the President down to the laborer; and there is no appeal from their decision. Public opinion may sometimes be unjust for a long time, especially in reference to politicians, but it hardly ever remains so, and there is no injury which it inflicts, which it is not in its power to remedy.

Another proof of the high premium at which morality is held in the United States consists in its influence on the elections of officers. In Europe, a man of genius is almost privileged. If he be a poet or an artist, allowances are made for the extravagance of his fancy, or the peculiarity of his appetites. If he be a statesman, his individual wanderings are forgotten for the general good he bestows on the nation; if he be a soldier, the wounds he may inflict upon virtue and unguarded innocence are pardoned for the sake of those he may have received in defending his country; and even the clergy have their offenses excused, in consideration of the morals which they promote by their spiritual functions. No such compensation takes place in the United States. Private virtue overtops the highest qualifications of the mind, and is indispensable to the progress even of the most acknowledged talents. This, in many instances, clips the wings of genius, by substituting a decent mediocrity in the place of brilliant but vicious talents; but the nation at large is nevertheless a gainer in the practice.

It must be remembered that the Americans are already in possession of most political advantages other nations are striving to obtain; and that their principal care, therefore, is rather to preserve what they have acquired than to enlarge their possessions; and for this purpose virtue and honest simplicity are infinitely preferable to the ambitious designs of towering talents. If morality, which is now the common law of the country, were once to be dispensed with in favor of certain individuals—if the exactions which are now made of every member of the community were to relax with regard to the peculiarly gifted, then the worst and most dangerous aristocracy would be introduced, which would not only shake the foundation of society, but eventually subvert the government. Talent, in a republic, must be valued principally in proportion as it is calculated to promote public good; every additional regard for it enriches only the possessor; and the Americans are too prudent a people to enrich and elevate individuals with the property and wealth of the nation.

The moment a candidate is presented for office, not only his mental qualifications for the functions he is about to assume, but also his private character are made the subject of criticism. Whatever he may have done, said, or listened to, from the time he left school to the present moment is sure to be brought before the public. The most trifling incidents which are calculated to shed a light on his motives or habits or thinking are made the subject of the most uncompromising scrutiny; and facts and circumstances, already buried in oblivion, are once more brought before the judging eye of the people. This, undoubtedly, gives rise to a vast deal of personal abuse and scurrility, and may even disturb the domestic peace of families; but then the candidates for office are comparatively few, while the people, who are to be benefited or injured by their election, are many; they are all presenting themselves of their own accord, and the people compelled to be their judges; they have friends to defend and extol their virtues, and they must therefore expect to have enemies, who will endeavor to tarnish their fair reputation. We may have pity on a repentant culprit—we may be roused to indignation by the condemnation of an innocent person; but we would not, on that account, abolish the trial by jury, or shut our courts of justice, which are instituted not only for the punishment but also for the prevention of crime. The process of an American election resembles that of a Roman canonization; the candidate must be fairly snatched from the clutches of the devil's advocate, before he can be admitted to the unrestrained enjoyment of paradise. If, in this manner, some are prevented from becoming saints, who have a just title to that dignity, it may also serve to prevent a heathen worship of idols, which would divert the people from the true faith.

It is an erroneous maxim, to consider American institutions as they are calculated to affect individuals: they are made for the people, and intended to benefit the majority. The consideration of quality must necessarily, in many instances, yield to the reflection on quantity; and a small benefit extended to large numbers, be preferred to a signal advantage conferred on a favored few. The American government, possessing little coercive power, cannot introduce sudden changes either for the better or worse, and is, therefore, less able to correct an abuse, if it is once introduced and sanctioned by the majority, than any other government in the world. It is consequently of the greatest importance that public morality should be preserved at any price, and that the people themselves should compose the tribunal before which the offenders are to be tried.

In Hochelaga; or, England in the New World, ed. Eliot Warburton (2 vols.; London, 1851), vol. 2, pp. 201-8, an anonymous English immigrant considered the apparent contradiction that although there were few "general signs of religious feeling among the American people," religion was nevertheless an essential ingredient to American democracy.

The first great point which we notice in the frame-work of American society, is, that it is without any provision for religion, as a State. Perhaps they consider their State so perfect that it has no necessity for connection with Christianity. In this respect they stand alone among the nations of the Christian world; England, France, and Russia may each be mistaken in the conviction of theirs being the only true Church; but they are all equally persuaded of the necessity of having some one or other to minister to the people: they, of course, choose that Church which they believe to be the true one, and assist it with temporal influence.

In America, no means are allotted for any system of religious education. The State, in some places, at least, pays very great attention to a boy's progress in arithmetic, that he may in due time become a useful money-making citizen; such an important matter as this could not be left to parental solicitude; but, as to mere matters of religion, the youth is allowed to pursue his own course unrestrictedly. The clergy are supported, like favourite actors, by the houses they draw, and by the gifts of their audience. In this, as in all other pursuits in this active country, there is a good deal of competition. In every considerable town there are many churches, devoted to a great variety of sects and shades of sects; there is no sort of influencing principle in the choice of that to be frequented: if the Presbyterian Church happen to have the most exciting preacher, its pews rapidly fill; if the Socinian be more fortunate, the result is the same for it.

All the pastors are elected by their congregations, and maintained as long as they please to keep them. The spiritual power is rarely used as a political engine, but in social life it acts very powerfully, particularly among women; this standing aloof from the turmoil of civil life is wise and proper. The Unitarian faith, as I mentioned elsewhere, generally comprises the most influential members of the community, the Episcopalian the most fashionable, the Presbyterian the most numerous, and the Roman Catholic, apparently, the most devout. The Episcopalian increases the most rapidly at present, by secession from others, over and above regular increase of population and by immigration.

Except in New England, I was much disappointed with the general signs of religious feeling among the American people. In the South, a great proportion of the men do not attend any divine service at all, and their habits and conversation are such as might be expected in consequence. It is said that, in the rural districts of New England, the manners and principles of their Puritan ancestors are still strong; and to their influence on the government of their States, is due to support of many of the severe ancient moral laws. In the original settlement of America, the men whose race has had the greatest share in leavening the now national character, were, undoubtedly, those who left the mother country from a determination to resist what they considred an unholy ecclesiastical authority, and for the sake of exercising free individual opinion in religion. In this they succeeded, and a similar disinclination to acknowledge any civil rules which did not emanate from themselves, was a natural consequence. This junction of religious feeling with a peculiar political tendency has given such an impetus to the latter, as to render it now irresistible.

The Irish Roman Catholics, a very numerous body in the States, who left their country during the action of the horrible Penal Laws, have, from their youth up, been accustomed to look upon any favoured classes as the enemies of their religion, and they have always thrown their full weight into the scale of extreme Democracy. Their union, more than their numbers, renders them at the present day the most important, in a political point of view, of the religious divisions.

The clergy in the United States, besides being well known to keep clear of party interests, exercise but little sectarian zeal even in attempts to proselytize; but their real influence is great and salutary: to them, in a most important degree, is due the barrier, still in many places remaining, between the extreme of rational liberty, and the anarchy and licence which lie beyond. By acting on the minds of a majority of individuals, in the cause of virtue, they enlist on its side the powers of government, which only represent the mind of this majority.

Although there is a very great number of churches in the United States, the actual accommodation in many of the thinly-peopled districts is, necessarily, but small: there is, also, a deficiency of ministers in proportion to the number of churches. The only source of income for the building of a church, and the support of its clergyman, being voluntarily supplied, the people who have, as they think, only sufficient for their temporal wants, and no particular care for their spiritual necessities, are left without any provision for the latter; and those who most stand in need of the offices of a minister of religion, are the very last to make any effort or sacrifice to obtain them. At the present time, the American people are nearly all so prosperous, that they can without difficulty supply themselves with assistance; but, as population increases, and as the value of labour and individual prosperity diminishes, the poor can have no resource. Already there are millions who have no place of public worship open to them at all.

As this state of things proceeds, the powerful incentive to virtue afforded by attendance at public worship, and by the example and instructions of their ministers, will cease to act upon individuals to the extent to which it now does; their majority may cease to be virtuous, and the powers of government will then be ranged against virtue. The immediate evil, however, of this voluntary system is, that its tendency is to silence the minister on the subject of any darling sin in his flock; far be it from me to say that this is always the result, but that such is its tendency there can be no doubt. Setting aside the pecuniary loss which the minister must undergo in being removed from his sacred office by a displeased congregation, he dreads it as destroying his means of being useful in his generation. He is thus tempted to adapt his words more to their tastes than their wants, and liable to follow, instead of directing, their spiritual course.

Religion, in America, in spite of the difficulties under which it labours, and the innumerable sects into which it is divided, is the ark of even its political salvation. Its professors, all meeting on the broad basis of Christian morality, predominate, at present, so decidedly, that in this strength is its safety; and no act of the government could take place directly and ostensibly contrary to religion or moral right. The wise among the Americans make certain efforts to prepare the minds of the people by the purification of religion, so as to enable them to bear free institutions, considering this the only safeguard from the threatened dangers by the latter. Happily for this great country, the interests of religion and of rational freedom, are indissolubly bound up together.

Though it was an important aspect of American society at large, American religion was sectarian and individualistic. According to Edward Dicey, a London journalist, an American's political prospects were totally independent of his religious affiliation. The following is taken from Dicey's article entitled "Religion in America," in Macmillan's Magazine, XV *(London, 1866), pp. 440-48.*

Even a very superficial observer, while travelling in America, can hardly avoid being struck by two remarkable and apparently inconsistent facts. Wherever you go, you see places of religious worship; every little town has meeting-houses, chapels, churches, conventicles by the score; the newest settlement, where houses are sufficiently numerous to form the semblance of a street, has some rough edifice of planks devoted, in one form or another, to spiritual purposes; the newspapers are filled with advertisements of sermons, chapel-feasts, prayer-meetings, and revivals; Sunday is observed with a more than English strictness; and, as far as outward signs go, the Americans would justly be set down as a very religious people. Yet, at the same time, you hear, I think, less about religion than you would in England. Everybody chooses his own religion,—it is thought right and proper for a man to be attached to some religious community; but, having made his selection, he is left undisturbed by his neighbours. Partisan religious controversy is therefore almost unknown in the form it is so common amongst us. Each sect is anxious enough to make proselytes and increase its numbers; but, under the voluntary system, all sects stand on exactly the same footing, and have a common interest in the universal toleration which protects them all. Thus religion is not an element in the political problem, as it is here. During a long period throughout which I have been in the habit of reading American newspapers, I can hardly recollect an instance where religious considerations have been introduced into the discussion of political matters. In this country, the creed professed by a public man is, to say the least, an important item in his prospects of success or failure. The religious persuasions to which our leading statesmen belong are as well known as the political principles they profess. That Mr. Bright is a Quaker, Sir George Bowyer a Catholic, Mr. Beresford Hope a High Churchman, Mr. Newdegate an Evangelical, and so on, are all facts which are, as it were, the A B C of political knowledge. But ninety-nine Americans out of a hundred could probably not tell you, to save their lives, the religious persuasions which owned the different members of the United States Government. In all the countless attacks which have been poured on President Lincoln, Johnson, Seward, Jefferson Davis, Wendell Phillips, and Charles Sumner, whoever heard an attack based upon their religious views? Yet I believe that one and all of these gentlemen would, in England, be called religious men,—that is, men to whom religion is professedly a matter of deep interest and importance. The truth is, that religion has grown to be considered in America entirely a matter appertaining to the individual, with which the State has no more concern than it has with his literary tastes or scientific pursuits. The only occasion in which religious partisanship was ever brought into a Presidential canvass was at the time of Fremont's election, when a cry was sought to be raised against him on the ground of his being a Catholic. But the apparent exception proves the rule: the only two religious denominations which have been in any sense made the objects of popular intolerance in the States are Roman Catholicism and Mormonism; and both these forms of faith are objected to, not on abstract grounds, but from a conviction, whether true or false, that their tenets are inconsistent with the principles on which the American Constitution is based. Thus, if my observation is correct, we have to account for the two somewhat contradictory facts that America is the country where religion flourishes in the greatest profusion, and yet where it has the least obvious connexion with the public life of the population.

In his visit to the United States in 1867-68, David Macrae was particularly interested in the active, voluntary nature of American religion. A Scottish Presbyterian minister, Macrae commented on clergymen and Sunday Schools in The Americans at Home: Pen-and-Ink Sketches of American Men, Manners, and Institutions *(Edinburgh, 1870), vol. 2, pp. 375-376, 382-384.*

In America a broader distinction is drawn between the Church and the world than here. In some denominations, nobody is called a Christian until he becomes a church member. I heard a lady say of her niece, "She is going to become a Christian next week." Membership in such cases means a great deal—the renunciation of much that is not forbidden to others, a higher profession, and the undertaking of some active Christian work. In many churches, the first question to a fresh communicant is, "What are you prepared to *do?* Can you visit the sick? Can you conduct a prayer-meeting? Can you teach in the Sunday-school?" and work is assigned accordingly. This develops Christian activity, and makes the Church a greater power for good. In religion, as in politics, the Americans are go-ahead, full of work, plans, and projects, preferring the risk of rushing into errors to the irksomeness of standing still.

The clergy occupy a somewhat different position in America from what they do in this country. There is no such distinction there as Churchman and Dissenter—no sect lifted up by the civil power to a position from which it can look down on others. The State secures to no American clergyman that glorious independence which a minister of the Establishment enjoys here, and which is always so comfortable a thing for his flock. The American clergyman, whether he be Presbyterian or Baptist, Episcopalian or Independent, has to depend entirely on his ability to supply the spiritual wants of his people. If he proves himself indisposed or unable to do that, no respect is shown him on account of his cloth; he is paid off with as little ceremony as a bungling lawyer or a useless clerk.

This dependence on the people has its disadvantages. It tends to make dumb dogs of many who would like to bark, and who see plenty to bark at, but who want the courage to offend the people on whom they depend for their salary. As a practical restraint, however, this acts far less than might be expected, as is evident from the fact, that

American ministers (like many ministers of Voluntary churches here) are found speaking out quite as boldly as any ministers of the Establishment. . . .

The great success of Sunday-schools in the States is partly due to the fact that the very best and most competent people in the church are amongst the teachers, including thousands of persons occupying high social positions. You find merchant-princes, generals, and Judges of the Supreme Court, as attentive to Sunday-school work as to their week-day employments. No work is considered nobler, or worthy of more careful study. I have lived with merchants who spent an hour every day in preparing for their Sunday-schools and classes. Is it wonderful that, with enthusiasm and serious preparation like this, these schools should have so far outstripped ours in efficiency and success?

The fact that common school education must be entirely, or almost entirely secular, and that the religious education of the young must depend on the parents and the Church, has greatly stimulated the movement, and invested it with a national importance. The Sunday-school teachers in each county meet regularly in convention, to arrange plans for the better working of the system; all these conventions send delegates to a convention for the State, and the conventions of the various States send delegates to the National Convention, which meets in Washington or Philadelphia, and which may be called the United States Sunday-School Congress. The movement is thus assuming rapidly the form of a great national system for the religious upbringing of the young. It is reckoned that 5,000,000 scholars are being trained in these schools. The Methodists alone have more than a million and a half of children in theirs.

Sunday observance in America is much the same as in England, with a few differences arising out of the peculiarities of the country. The steamers sail on the great lakes and rivers on Sunday and Saturday just as ours do on the open sea, a few trains run, and in all the cities the street-cars ply as usual—the distances in American towns being greater than in ours, and the Americans being very averse to long walks, especially in 90 degrees of summer heat, or 20 degrees of winter cold. Newspapers printed on Saturday night are published on Sunday, even in places where none are printed as ours are on Sunday to be published on Monday morning. Where the German element is strong the Sunday laws are laxer, and halls and pleasure-gardens are open, where the Teutons are wont to assemble, with their wives and little ones, to talk, smoke, drink lager-beer, and listen to music from an instrumental band. But over almost the whole continent, even in vast cities like New York, Philadelphia, and Chicago, business is suspended, and shops and public-houses closed—all this by the decision of the sovereign people legislating for themselves.

The circumstances of America have been in many respects peculiarly unfavourable to moral and spiritual development. There has been much in her history to foster the delusion that the regeneration of mankind may be accomplished through material comfort, free schools, and the ballot, with or without religion. And yet nowhere in the world has Christianity been making more progress. In 1800, when the population was 5,000,000, the church membership was 350,000; in 1860, when the population was 30,000,000, the church membership was found to have increased to 5,000,000. In other words, the proportion of avowed Christians to the entire population had far more than doubled—having increased from one in every fifteen to one in every six.

IV. EDUCATION, LARGE AND SMALL

By the mid-nineteenth century, most foreign visitors looked upon the American educational system with unbounded admiration. As Anthony Trollope, the English novelist, put it after observing our elementary schools in 1861, "it is almost impossible to mention them with too high praise." What aspects of American education were particularly noteworthy? What criticisms were made? What was the standard of judgment applied to education? What was it supposed to do, and for whom? How was education related to democracy? What lessons for Europe were drawn from the American system? How did American universities compare with European universities? What social classes primarily benefited from American education?

On his 1831 visit to America, Alexis de Tocqueville noted "How the Instruction, the Habits, and the Practical Experience of the Americans Promote the Success of their Democratic Institutions." Democracy in America, *translated by Henry Reeve (London, 1862), vol. 1, pp. 373-378.*

America has hitherto produced very few writers of distinction; it possesses no great historians, and not a single eminent poet. The inhabitants of that country look upon what are properly styled literary pursuits with a kind of disapprobation; and there are towns of very second-rate importance in Europe, in which more literary works are annually published, than in the twenty-four States of the Union put together. The spirit of the Americans is averse to general ideas; and it does not seek theoretical discoveries. Neither politics nor manufactures direct them to these occupations; and although new laws are perpetually enacted in the United States, no great writers have hitherto inquired into the general principles of their legislation. The Americans have lawyers and commentators, but no jurists; and they furnish examples rather than lessons to the world. The same observation applies to the mechanical arts. In America, the inventions of Europe are adopted with sagacity; they are perfected, and adapted with admirable skill to the wants of the country. Manufactures exist, but the science of manufacture is not cultivated; and they have good work-men, but very few inventors. Fulton was obliged to proffer his services to foreign nations for a long time, before he was able to devote them to his own country.

The observer who is desirous of forming an opinion on the state of instruction amongst the Anglo-Americans, must consider the same object from two different points of view. If he only singles out the learned, he will be astonished to find how rare they are; but if he counts the ignorant, the American people will appear to be the most enlightened community in the world. The whole population, as I observed in another place, is situated between these two extremes.

In New England, every citizen receives elementary notions of human knowledge; he is moreover taught the doctrines and the evidences of his religion, the history of his country, and the leading features of its Constitution. In the States of Connecticut and Massachusetts, it is extremely rare to find a man imperfectly acquainted with all these things, and a person wholly ignorant of them is a sort of phaenomenon.

When I compare the Greek and Roman Republics with these American States; the manuscript libraries of the former, and their rude population, with the innumerable journals and the enlightened people of the latter; when I remember all the attempts which are made to judge the modern republics by the assistance of those of antiquity, and to infer what will happen in our time from what took place two thousand years ago, I am tempted to burn my books, in order to apply none but novel ideas to so novel a condition of society.

What I have said of New England must not, however, be applied indistinctly to the whole Union: as we advance towards the West or the South, the instruction of the people diminishes. In the States which are adjacent to the Gulf of Mexico, a certain number of individuals may be found, as in our own countries, who are devoid of the rudiments of instruction. But there is not a single district in the United States sunk in complete ignorance; and for a very simple reason: the peoples of Europe started from the darkness of a barbarous condition, to advance towards the light of civilization; their progress has been unequal; some of them have improved apace, whilst others have loitered in their course, and some have stopped, and are still sleeping upon the way.

Such has not been the case in the United States. The Anglo-Americans settled in a state of civilization, upon that territory which their descendants occupy; they had not to begin to learn, and it was sufficient for them not to forget. Now the children of these same Americans are the persons who, year by year, transport their dwellings into the wilds; and with their dwellings their acquired information and their esteem for knowledge. Education has taught them the utility of instruction, and has enabled them to transmit that instruction to their posterity. In the United States society has no infancy, but it is born in man's estate.

The Americans never use the word 'peasant,' because they have no idea of the peculiar class which that term denotes; the ignorance of more remote ages, the simplicity of rural life, and the rusticity of the villager have not been preserved amongst them; and they are alike unacquainted with the virtues, the vices, the coarse habits, and the simple graces of an early stage of civilization. At the extreme borders of the confederate States, upon the confines of society and of the wilderness, a population of bold adventurers have taken up their abode, who pierce the solitudes of the American woods, and seek a country there, in order to escape that poverty which awaited them in their native provinces. As soon as the pioneer arrives upon the spot which is to serve him for a retreat, he fells a few trees and builds a log-house. Nothing can offer a more miserable aspect than these isolated dwellings. The traveller who approaches one of them towards night-fall, sees the flicker of the hearth-flame through the chinks in the walls; and at night, if the wind rises, he hears the roof of boughs shake to and fro in the midst of the great forest trees. Who would not suppose that this poor hut is the asylum of rudeness and ignorance?

Yet no sort of comparison can be drawn between the pioneer and the dwelling which shelters him. Everything about him is primitive and unformed, but he is himself the result of the labour and the experience of eighteen centuries. He wears the dress, and he speaks the language of cities; he is acquainted with the past, curious of the future, and ready for argument upon the present; he is, in short, a highly civilized being, who consents, for a time, to inhabit the back-woods, and who penetrates into the wilds of the New World with the Bible, an axe, and a file of newspapers.

It is difficult to imagine the incredible rapidity with which public opinion circulates in the midst of these deserts. I do not think that so much intellectual intercourse takes place in the most enlightened and populous districts of France. It cannot be doubted that, in the United States, the instruction of the people powerfully contributes to the support of a democratic republic; and such must always be the case I believe, where instruction which awakens the understanding, is not separated from moral education which amends the heart. But I by no means exaggerate this benefit, and I am still further from thinking, as so many people do think in Europe, that men can be instantaneously made citizens by teaching them to read and write. True information is mainly derived from experience, and if the Americans had not been gradually accustomed to govern themselves, their book-learning would not assist them much at the present day.

I have lived a great deal with the people in the United States, and I cannot express how much I admire their experience and their good sense. An American should never be allowed to speak of Europe; for he will then probably display a vast deal of presumption and very foolish pride. He will take up with those crude and vague notions which are so useful to the ignorant all over the world. But if you question him respecting his own country, the cloud which dimmed his intelligence will immediately disperse; his language will become as clear and as precise as his thoughts. He will inform you what his rights are, and by what means he exercises them; he will be able to point out the customs which obtain in the political world. You will find that he is well acquainted with the rules of the administration, and that he is familiar with the mechanism of the laws. The citizen of the United States does not acquire his practical science and his positive notions from books; the instruction he has acquired may have prepared him for receiving those ideas, but it did not furnish them. The American learns to know the laws by participating in the act of legislation; and he ?akes a lesson in the forms of government, from governing. The great work of society is ever going on beneath his eyes, and, as it were, under his hands.

In the United States politics are the end and aim of education; in Europe its principal object is to fit men for private life. The interference of the citizens in public affairs is too rare an occurrence for it to be anticipated beforehand. Upon casting a glance over society in the two hemispheres, these differences are indicated even by its external aspect.

In Europe we frequently introduce the ideas and the habits of private life into public affairs; and as we pass at once from the domestic circle to the government of the State, we may frequently be heard to discuss the great interests of society in the same manner in which we converse with our friends. The Americans, on the other hand, transfuse the habits of public life into their manners in private; and in their country the jury is introduced into the games of schoolboys, and parliamentary forms are observed in the order of a feast.

Although most Europeans praised American education, critics could always be found. One who was as critical of education as of most other aspects of the New World was Frances Trollope, an English-woman who lived for a period in Cincinnati and wrote her impressions in 1832. The following comments are taken from her Domestic Manners of the Americans *(2 vols.; New York, 1894 ed.), vol. 2, pp. 176-78.*

Much is said about the universal diffusion of education in America, and a vast deal of genuine admiration is felt and expressed at the progress of mind throughout the Union. They believe themselves in all sincerity to have surpassed, to be surpassing; and to be about to surpass, the whole earth in the intellectual race. I am aware that not a single word can be said, hinting a different opinion, which will not bring down a transatlantic anathema on my head; yet the subject is too interesting to be omitted. Before I left England I remember listening, with much admiration, to an eloquent friend, who deprecated our system of public education, as confining the various and excursive faculties of our children to one beaten path, paying little or no attention to the peculiar powers of the individual.

This objection is extremely plausible, but doubts of its intrinsic value must, I think, occur to every one who has marked the result of a different system throughout the United States.

From every inquiry I could make, and I took much pains to obtain accurate information, it appeared that much is attempted, but very little beyond reading, writing, and book-keeping, is thoroughly acquired. Were we to read a prospectus of the system pursued in any of our public schools, and that of a first-rate seminary in America, we should be struck by the confined scholastic routine of the former, when compared to the varied and expansive scope of the latter; but let the examination go a little farther, and I believe it will be found that the old-fashioned school discipline of England has produced something higher, and deeper too, than that which roars so loud, and thunders in the index.

They will not afford to let their young men study till two or three and twenty, and it is therefore declared, *ex cathedrâ Americanâ*, to be unnecessary. At sixteen, often much earlier, education ends, and money-making begins; the idea that more learning is necessary than can be acquired by that time, is generally ridiculed as obsolete monkish bigotry; added to which, if the seniors willed a more prolonged discipline, the juniors would refuse submission. When the money-getting begins, leisure ceases, and all of lore which can be acquired afterwards, is picked up from novels, magazines, and newspapers.

At what time can the taste be formed? How can a correct and polished style, even of speaking, be acquired? or when can the fruit of the two thousand years of past thinking be added to the native growth of American intellect? These are the tools, if I may so express myself, which our elaborate system of school discipline puts into the hands of our scholars; possessed of these, they may use them in whatever direction they please afterwards, they can never be an incumbrance.

No people appear more anxious to excite admiration and receive applause than the Americans, yet none take so little trouble, or make so few sacrifices to obtain it. This may answer among themselves, but it will not with the rest of the world; individual sacrifices must be made, and national economy enlarged, before America can compete with the old world in taste, learning, and liberality.

Alexander Mackay, a Scotsman serving as a correspondent for the London Morning Chronicle, *traveled extensively in the United States in 1846 and 1847. In his three-volume account,* The Western World; or, Travels in the United States in 1846-47 *(London, 1849), vol. 3, pp. 225-27, 230-32, 237-38, he emphasized the centrality of education in a democratic society, the importance of state rather than federal organization, and the distinction between religious and secular education.*

There is much in the general polity of America to strike the stranger with surprise, but nothing more calculated to excite his admiration, than the earnestness with which education is there universally promoted by the State, as a matter in which the State has the most deep and lasting interest. The American government is one which shrinks not from investigation, but covets the intelligent scrutiny of all who are subjected to it. It is founded neither on force nor fraud, and seeks not, therefore, to ally itself with ignorance. Based upon the principle of right and justice, it seeks to league itself with intelligence and virtue. Its roots lie deep in the popular will, and in the popular sympathies is the chief source of its strength. It is its great object, therefore, to have that will controlled and those sympathies regulated by an enlightened judgment. It thus calls education to its aid, instead of treating it as its foe.

Let those, who will, deny that the tendencies of human nature are to good, this is the broad principle upon which the American system of government rests. There is a great difference between believing in the better impulses of our common nature, and cherishing an "idolatrous enthusiasm" for humanity. The founders of the American system kept the brighter side of human nature in view when they organized their polity, instead of acting chiefly with a view to its darker traits. They did not lose sight of the propensity to evil, which so universally finds a place in the divided heart of man, but they framed their system more with a view to the encouragement of virtue than the repression of vice. They had no blind faith in the supremacy

of good over evil in the moral nature of man, but they acted throughout upon the conviction that man's social and political condition had
much to do, although not every thing, with the development of his
moral character. The tendency to good may be cherished, the propensity to evil checked, by the position which a man is made to occupy
with regard to his fellows. A man's moral nature is not only evi-
denced, but also greatly influenced by his acts. Place him in a position
in which the temptations to evil are more potent than the stimulants
to good, and if he give way, his consequent familiarity with evil acts
increases the propensity to them. But surround him with better influences, and every time he yields to them he strengthens the higher
impulses of his nature. A man's conduct is thus not only the result
of his moral character, but it also, to some extent, influences it. And
what chiefly influences his conduct? The circumstances in which he
is placed. The great object of philanthropy and of sound policy in
the government of mankind should therefore be to mould these circumstances so as to stimulate to good, instead of being provocative to
evil. This was the great object after which the noble race of men,
who framed the American Constitution, honestly and earnestly
strained. They repudiated a system founded upon the principles of suspicion and resistance, and adopted one based upon those of confidence
and encouragement. Faith in, not idolatry of, human nature was thus
at the very foundation of the edifice which they reared; and they took
care, in arranging the superstructure, that that in which they trusted,
the tendency to good—which, however it may be sometimes
smothered in the individual, can never be obliterated from the heart
of man—should have every opportunity given it of justifying their confidence. The sympathies of ignorance are more with the evil than with
the better principle of our composite natures; and they made it a primary object of their policy to assail ignorance, in every form in which
it presented itself. The sympathies of intelligence, on the other hand,
are more with virtue than vice; and the universal promotion of education was made one of the main features of their governmental system.
They thus regarded education in its true light, not merely as something
which should not be neglected, but as an indispensable co-adjutor in
the work of consolidating and promoting their scheme. They had not
only cause to further education, but they had every reason to dread
ignorance. They have so still, and the institutions of America will

only be permanently consolidated, when intelligence, in a high stage of development, is homogeneous to the Union. The American government, founded upon the principle of mutual confidence, thus wisely takes care that education shall be promoted, as one of the essential conditions to the realisation of its hopes. Its success is thus identified with human elevation—it can only be defeated by the degradation of humanity. . . . .

In speaking of the close alliance formed between the American system and general education, let me be understood to refer to the system in its local, not its federal manifestation. The education of the people is not one of the subjects, the control over which has been conceded to the general government. There were two reasons why the different States reserved its management to themselves. The first was the difficulty of procuring a general fund for its support, without investing the general government with some power of local taxation, a course which would have been at war with some of the fundamental axioms of the whole system. The other was the impossibility of devising a general plan of education for a people, whose political being was characterised by so many diversities of circumstances, and who differed so essentially from each other in some of their institutions. The States, therefore, prudently reserved the management of the whole subject to themselves. The cause of education has not lost by this; the States, particularly those in the north, running with each other a race of generous emulation in their separate efforts to promote it.

In a country in which the Church has been wholly divorced from the State, it was to be expected that education would be divested of the pernicious trammels of sectarian influence. The Americans have drawn a proper distinction between secular and religious instruction, confining the Church to its own duties, and leaving the schools free in the execution of theirs. They have not fallen into the ridiculous error of supposing that education is "Godless," when it does not embrace theology. Education has both its secular and its religious elements. As men cannot agree as to the latter, let not the former, on which they are agreed, be prevented from expanding by unnecessarily combining them. Cannot a mathematical axiom be taught, without incorporating with it a theological dogma? Is it necessary, in order to rescue this branch of education from the charge of godlessness, that a child should be taught that it is with God's blessing that the three angles of a triangle are together equal to two right angles; or that two and two, *Deo volente*, make four, otherwise they might have made five? Suppose, then, that we had schools for teaching arithmetic and mathematics alone, would any sane man charge them with being godless, because they confined themselves to the teaching of such simple truths as that two and two make four, and that the three angles of a traingle are together equal to two right angles? And what holds good of a branch of secular education, holds good of it in its entirety. If mathematics can be taught without theology, so can reading and writing, grammar and geography; in short, every department of secular learning. This is the view which the Americans have generally taken of the subject, and they have shaped their course accordingly. They have left religion to fortify itself exclusively in the heart of man, whilst they have treated secular education as a matter which essentially concerned the State. Either the Church is fit for the performance of its own duties, or it is not. If it is not, it is high time that it were remodelled; if it is, there is no reason why it should call upon the school to undertake a part of its work. The school might, with the same propriety, call upon the Church to aid it in the work of secular instruction. They will both best acquit themselves of their responsibilities, when they are confined exclusively to their own spheres. In America they are so, and with the happiest results. The children of all denominations meet peaceably together, to learn the elements of a good ordinary education. Nobody dreams of their being rendered godless by the process. Their parents feel assured that, for their religious education, they can entrust them to the Church and the Sunday-school. . . .

The results of the general attention to popular education characteristic of American polity, are as cheering as they are obvious. It divorces man from the dominion of his mere instincts, in a country, the institutions of which rely for their maintenance upon the enlightened judgments of the public. Events may occur which may catch the multitude in an unthinking humour, and carry it away with them, or which may blind the judgment by flattering appeals to the passions of the populace; but on the great majority of questions of a social and political import which arise, every citizen is found to entertain an intelligent opinion. He may be wrong in his views, but he can always offer you reasons for them. In this, how favourably does he contrast with the unreasoning and ignorant multitudes in other lands! All Americans read and write. Such children and adults as are found incapable of doing either, are emigrants from some of the less favoured regions of the older hemisphere, where popular ignorance is but too frequently regarded as the best guarantee for the stability of political systems.

Anthony Trollope, an English novelist who visited the United States in 1861, commented on American education in his North America, *published in 1862. The following excerpt, taken from a modern edition edited by Donald Smalley and Bradford Allen Booth, copyright © 1951 by Alfred A. Knopf, pp. 266-69, is notable for a positive tone vastly different from the attitude expressed by Trollope's mother thirty years earlier.*

The one matter in which, as far as my judgment goes, the people of the United States have excelled us Englishmen, so as to justify them in taking to themselves praise which we cannot take to ourselves or refuse to them, is the matter of Education. In saying this I do not think that I am proclaiming anything disgraceful to America. To the Americans of the States was given the good fortune of beginning at the beginning. The French at the time of their revolution endeavoured to reorganize everything, and to begin the world again with new habits and grand theories; but the French as a people were too old for such a change, and the theories fell to the ground. But in the States, after their revolution, an Anglo-Saxon people had an opportunity of making a new State, with all the experience of the world before them; and to this matter of education they were from the first aware that they must look for their success. They did so; and unrivalled population, wealth, and intelligence have been the results; and with these, looking at the whole masses of the people,—I think I am justified in saying, —unrivalled comfort and happiness. It is not that you, my reader, to whom in this matter of education fortune and your parents have probably been bountiful, would have been more happy in New York than in London. It is not that I, who, at any rate, can read and write, have cause to wish that I had been an American. But it is this;—if you and I can count up in a day all those on whom our eyes may rest, and learn the circumstances of their lives, we shall be driven to conclude that nine-tenths of that number would have had a better life as Americans than they can have in their spheres as Englishmen. The States are at a discount with us now, in the beginning of this year of grace 1862; and Englishmen were not very willing to admit the above statement, even when the States were not at a discount. But I do not think that a man can travel through the States with his eyes open and not admit the fact. . . . They have begun at the beginning, and have so managed that every one may learn to read and write,—have so managed that almost every one does learn to read and write. With us this cannot now be done. Population had come upon us in masses too thick for management before we had as yet acknowledged that it would be a good thing that these masses should be educated. Prejudices, too, had sprung up, and habits, and strong sectional feelings, all antagonistic to a great national system of education. We are, I suppose, now doing all that we can do; but comparatively it is little. I think I saw some time since that the cost for gratuitous education, or education in part gratuitous, which had fallen upon the nation had already amounted to the sum of 800,000*l.*; and I think also that I read in the document which revealed to me this fact, a very strong opinion that Government could not at present go much further. But if this matter were regarded in England as it is regarded in Massachusetts,—or rather, had it from some prosperous beginning been put upon a similar footing, 800,000*l.* would not have been esteemed a great expenditure for free education simply in the city of London. In 1857 the public schools of Boston cost 70,000*l.*, and these schools were devoted to a population of about 180,000 souls. Taking the population of London at two-and-a-half millions, the whole sum now devoted to England would, if expended in the metropolis, make education there even cheaper than it is in Boston. In Boston during 1857 there were above 24,000 pupils at these public schools, giving more than one-eighth of the whole population. But I fear it would not be practicable for us to spend 800,000*l.* on the gratuitous education of London. Rich as we are, we should not know where to raise the money. In Boston it is raised by a separate tax. It is a thing understood, acknowledged, and made easy by being habitual,—as is our national debt. I do not know that Boston is peculiarly blessed, but I quote the instance as I have a record of its schools before me. At the three high schools in Boston at which the average of pupils is

526, about 13*l*. per head is paid for free education. The average price
per annum of a child's schooling throughout these schools in Boston
is about 3*l*. per annum. To the higher schools any boy or girl may
attain without any expense, and the education is probably as good
as can be given, and as far advanced. The only question is, whether
it is not advanced further than may be necessary. Here, as at New
York, I was almost startled by the amount of knowledge around me,
and listened, as I might have done, to an examination in theology
among young Brahmins. When a yound lad explained in my hearing
all the properties of the different levers as exemplified by the bones
of the human body, I bowed my head before him in unaffected humil-
ity. We, at our English schools, never got beyond the use of those
bones which he described with such accurate scientific knowledge. . . .

It is impossible to refrain from telling all this, and from making
a little innocent fun out of the super-excellencies of these schools;
but the total result on my mind was very greatly in their favour. And
indeed the testimony came in both ways. Not only was I called on
to form an opinion of what the men and women would become from
the education which was given to the boys and girls, but also to say
what must have been the education of the boys and girls from what
I saw of the men and women. Of course it will be understood that
I am not here speaking of those I met in society, or of their children,
but of the working people,—of that class who find that a gratuitous
education for their children is needful, if any considerable amount of
education is to be given. The result is to be seen daily in the whole
intercourse of life. The coachman who drives you, the man who
mends your window, the boy who brings home your purchases, the
girl who stitches your wife's dress,—they all carry with them sure
signs of education, and show it in every word they utter.

*The two aspects of the American educational system which im-
pressed foreigners most were its public and its secular character. Following his visit to the United States in 1867-68, David Macrae, a
minister from Scotland, wrote the following in his* Americans at Home:
Pen-and-Ink Sketches of American Men, Manners, and Institutions 2
vols.; *(Edinburgh, 1870), vol. 2, pp. 387-389, 396-398.*

Nothing in America excited my admiration more than the system of common schools. To form an idea of it as carried out in the North, suppose a fisherman's net spread out upon a lawn; suppose the lawn to be the States; suppose all the little squares made by the net to be the school sections into which the States are divided; you have there a bird's-eye view of the whole country as divided for educational purposes. Every little square has its public school or schools, where all the children in that section—the children of the poor as well as of the rich—can go, free of charge, and get a good English education. To the regular schools over this vast area, add a plentiful sprinkling of Grammar and High Schools also free; wherever there are centres of population add clusters of schools and colleges, and you have before you a picture of the provision made by America for the education of her people. It is a magnificent development of the old Scottish system of parochial schools and endowed colleges.

The system is supported by a school-tax imposed by the people upon themselves. In many places this tax amounts to a mere trifle, by reason of the large amount of land originally appropriated for school purposes and rising in value; and also by donations of money made by private persons. But even at the heaviest the school-tax is very much lighter than the burden we in this country have to bear in supporting a system much less successful. Each district taxes itself according to its wants, and regulates its educational affairs through a committee acting within the limits of the general laws affecting schools. It follows that in some States and townships the teachers are better paid, the schools better, and education carried to a higher point than in others. In many of the States, not only can the poorest child enter the Common School and get instruction in all the branches of an English education, but by passing the requisite examinations he can proceed from the Common School to the High School, and from the High School to the College, the State paying for his education from first to last.

As yet the system is only working itself towards completeness. It has failed in the larger cities to bring in the lowest class of children for want of a compulsory law; while, on the other hand, numerous private academies are supported by people who pay the tax gladly to support the public schools, but are, or profess to be, afraid to let their own children commingle with other classes. The great mass of

American children, however, are educated in the Common
Schools. . . .

*In the States, almost the whole system of Common School education
is carried out by female teachers, and yet nowhere perhaps in the
world are children educated so well.* It was from no belief in the
superior qualifications of women for this work that the present state
of things came about. It arose simply from the fact that women were
ready to undertake the work at lower salaries; and, having undertaken
it, proved so competent that they have been allowed to retain almost
a monopoly of it. Even in Canada the proportion of female teachers
is yearly increasing. The same change probably awaits us here. If so,
our girls will have to be specially educated for the work as they are
in the Normal Schools in Canada and the States; but when so educated
their superior qualifications for managing, refining, and training the
young are likely to be recognised, and a new and vast field opened
up for the employment of educated women. . . .

The religious difficulty which has kept us so long out of a national
system of education, has been practically settled by the Americans.
Their position is this,—That public money appropriated for public
education cannot justly be expended on sectarian education. If half
the people are Romanists and half are Protestants, it is unjust to take
Protestant money to build Romish schools, and equally unjust to take
Romish money to build Protestant schools. But if all parties are agreed
that it is desirable to have their children taught to read, write, and
cipher, here is a kind of education which, being desired by the whole
public, can justly be paid for out of the public purse. On this position
America has reared her system of common schools, which is putting
the mass of her people so far in advance of ours in point of education.
To say that religion shall not be taught there, is not to say that religion
is less important than writing or ciphering, but simply that the public
are at one on the subject of writing and ciphering, while they are
at variance on the subject of religion.

But if the public are so much agreed even in regard to creed, as
to wish that certain religious exercises should be engaged in, then
the introduction of such exercises involves no injustice, as it drives
away no section of the public. In most of the schools, both in Canada
and the States, the opening exercises include a portion of Scripture
(read without comment), the Ten Commandments, and the Lord's

Prayer. To prevent any class of the public from being excluded on this account from schools which they are paying to support, it is arranged that parents who object to their children being present at these exercises, shall notify the same to the Principal, who shall not require the presence of such children until after these exercises are over. So far as I could discover, scarcely any, except here and there a few Roman Catholics, were availing themselves of this exemption. In all the common schools I visited, the children of Catholics, Jews, Unitarians, and Infidels, joined with the children of Baptists and Presbyterians in offering up the Lord's Prayer and hearing the Scriptures read. In many schools and colleges it is further provided, that a classroom be assigned after hours to every denomination that desires it, in order that a minister of each denomination may gather the pupils connected with it into a class and instruct them in their own creed. But it has been found in almost all such cases, in spite of the outcry made about it beforehand, that the churches are content to let this opportunity go by, finding that they have ampler and far more satisfactory opportunities of giving religious instruction in the pulpit, the Sunday-school, and the family circle.

An agitation is now afoot in some cities to have religious teaching altogether discontinued in schools paid for out of public money. If this agitation should prove successful, the effect will simply be, that public schools will be confined to their proper work, while churches and parents will be made to feel the responsibility of providing religious education—a duty which America has already declared in principle belongs to them, not to the State.

The term "secular education" may be a convenient name for education that does not trench on religious ground; but to use the term in an opprobrious sense as equivalent to infidel education, looks like the blunder of an idiot or the sophistry of a partisan. Nobody speaks of secular arithmetic, or secular gymnastics. Nobody speaks of the Lighting and Paving Act as a secular and infidel measure, because it provides for the streets being cleaned without requiring the scavengers to sign the Confession of Faith. Nobody speaks of a riding-school as secular, because the pupils are taught horsemanship without the Catechism. And yet the term would be just as applicable to them as to common schools established for the purpose of teaching children to read, write, and cipher, and confining themselves to this work, leaving religion to be taught properly by those to whom the religious education of the people properly belongs.

Toward the end of the nineteenth century, Europeans became interested in American higher education. One commentator, James Bryce, had himself been educated at three of the finest institutions in the Old World (Glasgow, Oxford, and Heidelburg), and from 1870 to 1893 served as the Regius Professor of Civil Law at Oxford. An English lawyer, professor, and politician, Bryce visited the United States several times between 1870 and 1887. Upon his return in 1905, he wrote "America Revisited: The Changes of a Quarter-Century" for The Outlook *(1905). His comments on American universities are found on pp. 736-38 of that essay.*

There has been within these last thirty-five years a development of the higher education in the United States perhaps without a parallel in the world. Previously the Eastern States had but a very few universities whose best teachers were on a level with the teachers in the universities of western Europe. There were a great many institutions bearing the name of universities over the Northern and Middle States and the West, and a smaller number in the South, but they gave an instruction which, though in some places (and especially in New England) it was sound and thorough as far as it went, was really the instruction rather of a secondary school than of a university in the proper sense. In the West and South the teaching, often ambitious when it figured in the program, was apt to be superficial and flimsy, giving the appearance without the solid reality of knowledge. The scientific side was generally even weaker than the literary. These universities and colleges had their value, for their very existence was a recognition of the need for an education above that which the school is intended to supply. I ventured even then to hazard the opinion that the reformers who wished to extinguish the bulk of them or to turn them into schools, reserving the degree-granting power to a selected few only, were mistaken, because improvement and development might be expected. But I did not expect that the development would come so fast and go so far. No doubt there are still a great many whose standard of teaching and examination is that of a school, not of a true university. But there are also many which have risen to the European level, and many others which are moving rapidly towards it. Roughly speaking—for it is impossible to speak with exactness —America now has not less than fifteen or perhaps even twenty seats of learning fit to be ranked beside the universities of Germany, France, and England as respects the completeness of the instruction which they provide and the thoroughness at which they aim. Only a few have a professorial staff containing names equal to those which adorn the faculties of Berlin and Leipzig and Vienna, of Oxford, Cambridge, Edinburgh, and Glasgow. Men of brilliant gifts are scarce in all countries, and in America there has hardly been time to produce a supply equal to the immense demand for the highest instruction which has lately shown itself. It is the advance in the standard aimed at, and in the efforts to attain that standard, that is so remarkable. Even more noticeable is the amplitude of the provision now made for the study of the natural sciences and of those arts in which science is applied to practical ends. In this respect the United States has gone ahead of Great Britain, aided no doubt by the greater pecuniary resources which not a few of her universities possess, and which they owe to the wise liberality of private benefactors. In England nothing is so hard as to get money from private persons for any educational purpose. Mr. Carnegie's splendid gift to the universities of Scotland stands almost alone. In America nothing is so easy. There is, indeed, no better indication of the prosperity of the country and of its intelligence than the annual record of the endowments bestowed on the universities by successful businessmen, some of whom have never themselves had more than a common school education. Only in one respect does that poverty which Europe has long associated with learning reappear in America. The salaries of presidents and professors remain low as compared with the average income of persons in the same rank, and as compared with the cost of living. That so many men of an energy and ability sufficient to win success and wealth in a business career do nevertheless devote themselves to a career of teaching and research is a remarkable evidence of the intellectual zeal which pervades the people.

The improvement in the range and quality of university teaching is a change scarcely more remarkable than the increased afflux of students. It seems (for I have not worked the matter out in figures, as

I am giving impressions and not statistics) to have grown much faster than population has grown, and to betoken an increased desire among parents and young men to obtain a complete intellectual equipment for life. The number of undergraduates at Harvard is much larger than is the number who resort to Oxford; the number at Yale is larger than the number at Cambridge (England). Five leading universities of the Eastern States—Harvard, Yale, Columbia, Princeton, Pennsylvania—count as many students as do all the universities of England (omitting in both cases those who attend evening classes only), although there are twice as many universities in England now as there were forty years ago, and although the English students have much more than doubled in number. And whereas in England the vast majority go to prepare themselves for some profession—law, journalism, medicine, engineering, or the ministry of the Established Church—there is in America a considerable proportion (in one institution I heard it reckoned at a third or more) who intend to choose a business career, such as manufacturing, or banking, or commerce, or railroading. In England nearly every youth belonging to the middle and upper class who takes to business goes into a commercial office or workshop not later than seventeen. In the United States, if he graduates at a university, he continues his liberal education till he is twenty-one or twenty-two. This practical people do not deem these three years lost time. They believe that the young man is all the more likely to succeed in business if he goes into it with a mind widely and thoroughly trained. To say that the proportion of college graduates to the whole population is larger in America than in any European country would not mean much, because graduation from a good many of the colleges means very little. But if we take only those colleges which approach or equal the West European standard, I think the proportion will be as high as it is in Germany or Switzerland or Scotland and higher than it is in England.

This feature of recent American development has an important bearing on the national life. It is a counterpoise to the passion, growing always more intense, for material progress, to the eagerness to seize every chance, to save every moment, to get the most out of every enterprise. . . . It adds to the number of those who may find some occasion in their business life for turning a knowledge of natural sci-

themselves. Nor is its social influence to be overlooked. One is frequently impressed in America by the attachment of the graduates to the place of their education, by their interest in its fortunes, by their willingness to respond when it asks them for money. In great cities there are always university clubs, and in some cities these clubs have become centers for social and political action for good public ends. Not infrequently they take the lead in municipal reform movements.

V. AMERICANS AT WORK

European travelers agreed that Americans worked extremely hard. As Francis Grund noted in 1837, Americans considered work "as essential to their well-being as food and raiment to a European." They assumed that work was good and that good citizens worked hard. "The Americans are restless," the English poet and essayist Matthew Arnold commented in 1884, "eager to better themselves and to make fortunes." Why did Americans work so hard? What bearing did such strenuous activity seem to have on the development of mental and cultural values in the United States? Why was America a "land of pressure" as well as a land of opportunity? Was work an end in itself for Americans, or was it a means to an end? What types of workers do each of these commentators seem to be speaking about—farmers, factory workers, or businessmen?

Early in the nineteenth century, most Americans still lived and worked on farms. And there they worked hard indeed, according to William Cobbett, himself an English farmer, author, and politician who lived in the United States from 1792 to 1800, and again for a year in 1817. Cobbett's comments are to be found in the ninth chapter of A Year's Residence the United States of America, *published originally in 1818. The following is taken from a more recent edition entitled* A Years Residence in America *(London, c. 1900), pp. 142-45.*

It is of importance to know, *what sort* of labourers these Americans are; for, though a labourer is a labourer, still there is some difference in them; and, these Americans are *the best that I ever saw*. They mow *four acres* of *oats, wheat, rye,* or *barley* in a day, and, with a cradle, lay it so smooth in the swarths, that it is tied up in sheaves with the greatest neatness and ease. They mow *two acres and a half of grass* in a day, and they do the work well. And the crops, upon an average, are all, except the wheat, *as heavy* as in England. The English farmer will want nothing more than these facts to convince him, that the labour, after all, is not so *very dear*.

The causes of these performances, so far beyond those in England, is first, the men are *tall* and well built; they are *bony* rather than *fleshy*: and they *live*, as to food, as well as man can live. And, secondly, they have been *educated* to do much in a day. The farmer here generally is at the *head* of his *"boys"* as they, in the kind language of the country, are called. Here is the best of examples. My old and beloved friend, MR. JAMES PAUL, used, at the age of nearly *sixty* to go at *the head of his mowers*, though his fine farm was his own, and though he might, in other respects, be called a rich man; and, I have heard, that MR. ELIAS HICKS, the famous Quaker Preacher, who lives about nine miles from this spot, has this year, at *seventy* years of age, cradled down four acres of rye a day. I wish some of the *preachers* of other descriptions, especially our fat parsons in England, would think a little of this, and would betake themselves to "work with their hands the things which be good, that they may have to give to him who needeth," and not go any longer gormandizing and swilling upon the labour of those who need.

Besides the great quantity of work performed by the American labourer, his *skill*, the *versatility* of his talent, is a great thing. Every man can use an *ax*, a *saw*, and a *hammer*. Scarcely one who cannot do any job at rough carpentering, and mend a plough or a waggon. Very few indeed, who cannot kill and dress pigs and sheep, and many of them Oxen and Calves. Every farmer is a *neat* butcher; a butcher for *market*: and, of course, "the boys" must learn. This is a great convenience. It makes you so independent as to a main part of the means of housekeeping. All are *ploughmen*. In short, a good labourer here, can do *any thing* that is to be done upon a farm.

The operations necessary in miniature cultivation they are very awkward at. The *gardens are ploughed* in general. An American labourer uses a *spade* in a very awkward manner. They *poke the earth about* as if they had no eyes; and toil and muck themselves half to death to dig as much ground in a day as a Surrey man would dig in about an hour of hard work. *Banking, hedging,* they know nothing about. They have no idea of the use of a *bill-hook,* which is so adroitly used in the coppices of Hampshire and Sussex. An *ax* is their tool, and with that tool, at *cutting down* trees or *cutting them up,* they will do *ten times* as much in a day as any other men that I ever saw. Set one of these men on upon a wood of timber trees, and his slaughter will astonish you. A neighbour of mine tells a story of an Irishman, who promised he could *do any thing,* and whom, therefore, to begin with, the employer sent into the wood to cut down a load of wood to burn. He staid a long while away with the team, and the farmer went to him fearing some accident had happened. "What are you about all this time?" said the farmer. The man was hacking away at a hickory tree, but had not got it half down; and that was all he had done. An American, black or white, would have had half a dozen trees cut down, cut up into lengths, put upon the carriage, and brought home, in the time.

So that our men, who come from England must not expect, that, in these *common labours* of the country, they are to surpass, or even equal these "*Yankees,*" who, of all men that I ever saw, are the most *active* and the most *hardy.* They skip over a fence like a greyhound. They will catch you a pig in an open field by *racing* him down; and they are afraid of nothing. . . .

An American labourer is not regulated, as to time, by *clocks* and *watches.* The *sun,* who seldom hides his face, tells him when to begin in the morning and when to leave off at night. He has a dollar, a *whole dollar* for his work; but then it is the work of a *whole day.* Here is no dispute about *hours.* "*Hours* were made for *slaves,*" is an old saying; and, really, they seem here to act upon it as a practical maxim. This is a *great thing* in agricultural affairs. It prevents so many disputes. It removes so great a cause of disagreement. The American labourers, like the tavern-keepers, are never *servile,* but always *civil.* Neither *boobishness* nor *meanness* mark their character. They never *creep* and *fawn,* and are never *rude.* Employed about your house as day-labourers, they never come to interlope for victuals or drink. They have no idea of such a thing: Their pride would restrain them if their plenty did not; and, thus would it be with all labourers, in all countries, were they left to enjoy the fair produce of their labour. Full pocket or empty pocket, these American labourers are always the *same men;* no saucy cunning in the one case, and no base crawling in the other. This, too, arises from the free institutions of government. A man has a voice *because he is a man,* and not because he is the *possessor of money.* And, shall I *never* see our English labourers in this happy state?

Let those English farmers, who love to see a poor wretched labourer stand trembling before them with his hat off, and who think no more of him than of a dog, remain where they are; or, go off, on the cavalry horses, to the devil at once, if they wish to avoid the tax-gatherer; for, they would, here, meet with so many mortifications, that they would, to a certainty, hang themselves in a month.

There are some, and even many, farmers, who *do not work themselves in the fields.* But, they all *attend* to the thing, and are all equally civil to their working people. They manage their affairs very judiciously. Little talking. Orders plainly given in few words, and in a decided tone. This is their only secret.

The *cattle* and *implements* used in husbandry are cheaper than in England; that is to say, *lower priced.* The wear and tear not nearly half so much as upon a farm in England of the same size. The climate, the soil, the gentleness and docility of the horses and oxen, the lightness of the waggons and carts, the lightness and toughness of the *wood* of which husbandry implements are made, the simplicity of the harness, and, above all, the ingenuity and handiness of the workmen in *repairing,* and in *making shift:* all these make the implements a matter of very little note. Where horses are kept, the *shoing* of them is the most serious kind of expence.

The first business of a farmer is, here, and ought to be every where, to *live well;* to live in ease and plenty; to "*keep hospitality,*" as the old English saying was. To *save money* is a secondary consideration; but, any English farmer, who is a good farmer there, may, if he will bring his industry and care with him, and be *sure* to leave his pride and insolence (if he have any) along with his anxiety, behind him, live in ease and plenty here, and keep hospitality, and save a great parcel of money too.

Alexis de Tocqueville's explanation for "Why the Americans Are So Restless in the Midst of their Prosperity" is taken from Democracy in America, *translated by Henry Reeve (London, 1862), vol. 2, pp. 161-165.*

In certain remote corners of the Old World you may still sometimes stumble upon a small district which seems to have been forgotten amidst the general tumult, and to have remained stationary whilst everything around it was in motion. The inhabitants are for the most part extremely ignorant and poor; they take no part in the business of the country, and they are frequently oppressed by the government; yet their countenances are generally placid, and their spirits light.

In America I saw the freest and most enlightened men, placed in the happiest circumstances which the world affords: it seemed to me as if a cloud habitually hung upon their brow, and I thought them serious and almost sad even in their pleasures.

The chief reason of this contrast is that the former do not think of the ills they endure,—the latter are for ever brooding over advantages they do not possess. It is strange to see with what feverish ardour the Americans pursue their own welfare; and lest they should not have chosen the shortest path which may lead to it.

A native of the United States clings to this world's goods as if he were certain never to die; and he is so hasty in grasping at all within his reach, that one would suppose he was constantly afraid of not living long enough to enjoy them. He clutches everything, he holds nothing fast, but soon loosens his grasp to pursue fresh gratifications.

In the United States a man builds a house to spend his latter years in it, and he sells it before the roof is on: he plants a garden, and lets it just as the trees are coming into bearing: he brings a field into tillage, and leaves other men to gather the crops: he embraces a profession, and gives it up: he settles in a place, which he soon afterwards leaves, to carry his changeable longings elsewhere. If his private affairs leave him any leisure, he instantly plunges into the vortex of politics; and if at the end of a year of unremitting labour he finds he has a few days' vacation, his eager curiosity whirls him over the vast extent of the United States, and he will travel fifteen hundred miles in a few days, to shake off his happiness. Death at length overtakes him, but it is before he is weary of his bootless chase of that complete felicity which is for ever on the wing.

At first sight there is something surprising in this strange unrest of so many happy men, restless in the midst of abundance. The spectacle itself is however as old as the world; the novelty is to see a whole people furnish an exemplification of it.

Their taste for physical gratifications must be regarded as the original source of that secret inquietude which the actions of the Americans betray, and of that inconstancy of which they afford fresh examples every day. He who has set his heart exclusively upon the pursuit of worldly welfare is always in a hurry, for he has but a limited time at his disposal to reach it, to grasp it, and to enjoy it. The recollection of the brevity of life is a constant spur to him. Besides the good things which he possesses, he every instant fancies a thousand others which death will prevent him from trying if he does not try them soon. This thought fills him with anxiety, fear, and regret, and keeps his mind in ceaseless trepidation, which leads him perpetually to change his plans and his abode.

If an addition to the taste for physical well-being a social condition be superadded, in which the laws and customs make no condition permanent, here is a great additional stimulant to this restlessness of temper. Men will then be seen continually to change their track, for fear of missing the shortest cut to happiness.

It may readily be conceived, that if men, passionately bent upon physical gratifications, desire eagerly, they are also easily discouraged: as their ultimate object is to enjoy, the means to reach that object must be prompt and easy, or the trouble of acquiring the gratification would be greater than the gratification itself. Their prevailing frame of mind then is at once ardent and relaxed, violent and enervated. Death is often less dreaded than perseverance in continuous efforts to one end.

The equality of conditions leads by a still straighter road to several of the effects which I have here described. When all the privileges of birth and fortune are abolished, when all professions are accessible to all, and a man's own energies may place him at the top of any one of them, an easy and unbounded career seems open to his ambition, and he will readily persuade himself that he is born to no vulgar destinies. But this is an erroneous notion, which is corrected by daily experience. The same equality which allows every citizen to conceive these lofty hopes, renders all the citizens less able to realize them: it circumscribes their powers on every side, whilst it gives freer scope to their desires. Not only are they themselves powerless, but they are met at every step by immense obstacles, which they did not at first perceive. They have swept away the privileges of some of their fellow creatures which stood in their way; but they have opened the door to universal competition: the barrier has changed its shape rather than its position. When men are nearly alike, and all follow the same track, it is very difficult for any one individual to walk quick and cleave a way through the dense throng which surrounds and presses him. This constant strife between the propensities springing from the equality of conditions and the means it supplies to satisfy them, harasses and wearies the mind.

It is possible to conceive men arrived at a degree of freedom which should completely content them; they would then enjoy their independence without anxiety and without impatience. But men will never establish any equality with which they can be contented. Whatever efforts a people may make, they will never succeed in reducing all the conditions of society to a perfect level; and even if they unhappily attained that absolute and complete depression, the inequality of minds would still remain, which, coming directly from the hand of God, will for ever escape the laws of man. However democratic then the social state and the political constitution of a people may be, it is certain that every member of the community will always find out several points about him which command his own position; and we may foresee that his looks will be doggedly fixed in that direction. When inequality of conditions is the common law of society, the most marked inequalities do not strike the eye: when everything is nearly on the same level, the slightest are marked enough to hurt it. Hence the desire of equality always becomes more insatiable in proportion as equality is more complete.

Amongst democratic nations men easily attain a certain equality of conditions: they can never attain the equality they desire. It perpetually retires from before them, yet without hiding itself from their sight, and in retiring draws them on. At every moment they think they are about to grasp it; it escapes at every moment from their hold. They are near enough to see its charms, but too far off to enjoy them; and before they have fully tasted its delights, they die.

To these causes must be attributed that strange melancholy which oftentimes will haunt the inhabitants of democratic countries in the midst of their abundance, and that disgust at life which sometimes seizes upon them in the midst of calm and easy circumstances. Complaints are made in France that the number of suicides increases; in America suicide is rare, but insanity is said to be more common than anywhere else. These are all different symptoms of the same disease. The Americans do not put an end to their lives, however disquieted they may be, because their religion forbids it; and amongst them materialism may be said hardly to exist, notwithstanding the general passion for physical gratification. The will resists,—reason frequently gives way.

In democratic ages enjoyments are more intense than in the ages of aristocracy, and especially the number of those who partake in them is larger: but, on the other hand, it must be admitted that man's hopes and his desires are oftener blasted, the soul is more stricken and perturbed, and care itself more keen.

Most foreign visitors saved their comments on American society until they went home to write an account of their travels for publication. But not Herbert Spencer, the English "Social Darwinist" whose writings were read widely in the United States before he himself came for a short visit in 1882. Just before he returned to England, a banquet was given in his honor in New York City. Asked to speak, Spencer shocked his audience by addressing himself to the apparent tendency of Americans to work too hard. The following portion of his speech is reprinted by permission of Hawthorn Books, Inc. from Volume 3 of Essays, Scientific, Political and Speculative *by Herbert Spencer, vol.3, pp. 481-86. All rights reserved.*

Already, in some remarks drawn from me respecting American

affairs and American character, I have passed criticisms, which have been accepted far more good-humouredly than I could have reasonably expected; and it seems strange that I should now propose again to transgress. However, the fault I have to comment upon is one which most will scarcely regard as a fault. It seems to me that in one respect Americans have diverged too widely from savages, I do not mean to say that they are in general unduly civilized. Throughout large parts of the population, even in long-settled regions, there is no excess of those virtues needed for the maintenance of social harmony. Especially out in the West, men's dealings do not yet betray too much of the "sweetness and light" which we are told distinguish the cultured man from the barbarian. Nevertheless, there is a sense in which my assertion is true. You know that the primitive man lacks power of application. Spurred by hunger, by danger, by revenge, he can exert himself energetically for a time; but his energy is spasmodic. Monotonous daily toil is impossible to him. It is otherwise with the more developed man. The stern discipline of social life has gradually increased the aptitude for persistent industry; until, among us, and still more among you, work has become with many a passion. This contrast of nature has another aspect. The savage thinks only of present satisfactions, and leaves future satisfactions uncared for. Contrariwise, the American, eagerly pursuing a future good, almost ignores what good the passing day offers him; and when the future good is gained, he neglects that while striving for some still remoter good.

What I have seen and heard during my stay among you has forced on me the belief that this slow change from habitual inertness to persistent activity has reached an extreme from which there must begin a counterchange—a reaction. Everywhere I have been struck with the number of faces which told in strong lines of the burdens that had to be borne. I have been struck, too, with the large proportion of gray-haired men; and inquiries have brought out the fact, that with you the hair commonly begins to turn some ten years earlier than with us. Moreover, in every circle I have met men who had themselves suffered from nervous collapse due to stress of business, or named friends who had either killed themselves by overwork, or had been permanently incapacitated, or had wasted long periods in endeavors to recover health. I do but echo the opinion of all the observant persons I have spoken to, that immense injury is being done by this high-pressure life—the physique is being undermined. That subtle thinker and poet whom you have lately had to mourn, Emerson, says, in his essay on the Gentleman, that the first requisite is that he shall be a good animal. The requisite is a general one—it extends to the man, to the father, to the citizen. We hear a great deal about "the vile body;" and many are encouraged by the phrase to transgress the laws of health. But Nature quietly suppresses those who treat thus disrespectfully one of her highest products, and leaves the world to be peopled by the descendants of those who are not so foolish.

Beyond these immediate mischiefs there are remoter mischiefs. Exclusive devotion to work has the result that amusements cease to please; and, when relaxation becomes imperative, life becomes dreary from lack of its sole interest—the interest in business. The remark current in England that, when the American travels, his aim is to do the greatest amount of sight-seeing in the shortest time, I find current here also: it is recognized that the satisfaction of getting on devours nearly all other satisfactions. When recently at Niagara, which gave us a whole week's pleasure, I learned from the landlord of the hotel that most Americans come one day and go away the next. Old Froissart, who said of the English of his day that "they take their pleasures sadly after their fashion," would doubtless, if he lived now, say of the Americans that they take their pleasures hurriedly after their fashion. In large measure with us, and still more with you, there is not that abandonment to the moment which is requisite for full enjoyment; and this abandonment is prevented by the ever-present sense of multitudinous responsibilities. So that, beyond the serious physical mischief caused by overwork, there is the further mischief that it destroys what value there would otherwise be in the leisure part of life.

Nor do the evils end here. There is the injury to posterity. Damaged constitutions reappear in children, and entail on them far more of ill than great fortunes yield them of good. When life has been duly rationalized by science, it will be seen that among a man's duties, care of the body is imperative; not only out of regard for personal welfare, but also out of regard for descendants. His constitution will be considered as an entailed estate, which he ought to pass on uninjured, if not improved, to those who follow; and it will be held that millions bequeathed by him will not compensate for feeble health and decreased ability to enjoy life. Once more, there is the injury to fellow-citizens, taking the shape of undue disregard of competitors. I hear that a great trader among you deliberately endeavoured to crush out every one whose business competed with his own; and manifestly the man who, making himself a slave to accumulation, absorbs an inordinate share of the trade or profession he is engaged in, makes life harder for all others engaged in it, and excludes from it many who might otherwise gain competencies. Thus, besides the egoistic motive, there are two altruistic motives which should deter from this excess in work.

The truth is, there needs a revised ideal of life. Look back through the past, or look abroad through the present, and we find that the ideal of life is variable, and depends on social conditions. Every one knows that to be a successful warrior was the highest aim among all ancient peoples of note, as it is still among many barbarous peoples. When we remember that in the Norseman's heaven the time was to be passed in daily battles, with magical healing of wounds, we see how deeply rooted may become the conception that fighting is man's proper business, and that industry is fit only for slaves and people of low degree. That is to say, when the chronic struggles of races necessitate perpetual wars, there is evolved an ideal of life adapted to the requirements. We have changed all that in modern civilized societies; especially in England, and still more in America. With the decline of militant activity, and the growth of industrial activity, the occupations once disgraceful have become honourable. The duty to work has taken the palce of the duty to fight; and in the one case, as in the other, the ideal of life has become so well established that scarcely any dream of questioning it. Practically, business has been substituted for war as the purpose of existence.

Is this modern ideal to survive throughout the future? I think not. While all other things undergo continuous change, it is impossible that ideals should remain fixed. The ancient ideal was appropriate to the ages of conquest by man over man, and spread of the strongest races. The modern ideal is appropriate to ages in which conquest of the earth and subjection of the powers of Nature to human use, is the predominant need. But hereafter, when both these ends have in the main been achieved, the ideal formed will probably differ considerably from the present one. May we not foresee the nature of the differences? I think we may. Some twenty years ago, a good friend of mine, and a good friend of yours too, though you never saw him, John Stuart Mill, delivered at St. Andrews an inaugural address on the occasion of his appointment to the Lord Rectorship. It contained much to be admired, as did all he wrote. There ran through it, however, the tacit assumption that life is for learning and working. I felt at the time that I should have liked to take up the opposite thesis. I should have liked to contend that life is not for learning, nor is life for working, but learning and working are for life. The primary use of knowledge is for such guidance of conduct under all circumstances as shall make living complete. All other uses of knowledge are secondary. It scarcely needs saying that the primary use of work is that of supplying the materials and aids to living completely; and that any other uses of work are secondary. But in men's conceptions the secondary has in great measure usurped the place of the primary. The apostle of culture as it is commonly conceived, Mr. Matthew Arnold, makes little or no reference to the fact that the first use of knowledge is the right ordering of all actions; and Mr. Carlyle, who is a good exponent of current ideas about work, insists on its virtues for quite other reasons that that it achieves sustentation. We may trace everywhere in human affairs a tendency to transform the means into the end. All see that the miser does this when, making the accumulation of money his sole satisfaction, he forgets that money is of value only to purchase satisfactions. But it is less commonly seen that the like is true of the work by which the money is accumulated—that industry too, bodily or mental, is but a means; and that it is as irrational to pursue it to the exclusion of that complete living it subserves, as it is for the miser to accumulate money and make no use of it. Hereafter, when this age of active material progress has yielded mankind its benefits, there will, I think, come a better adjustment of labour and enjoyment. Among reasons for thinking this, there is the reason that the process of evolution throughout the organic world at large, brings an increasing surplus of energies that are not absorbed in fulfilling material needs, and points to a still larger surplus for the humanity of the future. And there are other reasons, which I must pass over. In brief, I may say that we have had somewhat too much of "the gospel of work." It is time to preach the gospel of relaxation.

The work ethic or business mentality, was at the heart of nineteenth-century American life, according to G. W. Steevens, a correspondent for the London Daily Mail *who came to the United States in 1896. In* The Land of the Dollar *(Edinburgh and London, 1897), pp. 264-65, 271-73, Steevens noted the beneficial as well as the harmful aspects of this mentality.*

Business is business all the world over; so, at least, I have been assured by those who ought to know. But it is more emphatically business in the United States than anywhere else. In England business is business, and there's an end of it; here business is everything, and there is no end or boundary to it. It affords the one career in the country. Politics is a matter that a citizen must interest himself in one year out of four; but the class which pursues politics day by day and week by week is a small one, and neither very respectable nor very respected. The Church, literature, art, the services—they may be all very excellent things in their way if anybody has the curious fancy to make a life of them. But they are hardly regarded as serious careers. The leading men, go where you will—the show citizens that your hospitable entertainer gives you introductions to—are not any of these; they are the first men of business. The first men of business are the first men outright. . . .

What is the effect of this universality of business in America? It has its murderous side, as we have seen. The weak men who go down are not pitied, and especially not respected. They are dead failures. In Europe there remain some kindly superstitions under which the unsuccessful may take refuge from public contempt. A man may be incompetent, but after all he is of good family; he is well educated; he is a fine musician; he is a witty fellow. But in America the man who fails in business has failed in the one thing there is to do. The one test of worth in business is to make money, for that is the object of business. Failing in that, his failure is absolute.

But there is another side. In the first place, the pre-eminence of business is a great clip that holds this unwieldy country together. An active man of business will have interests in every quarter of the States. These interests compel him to know every part of the country, its economic conditions, the habits, pursuits, and character of its inhabitants. But for this bond I verily believe the Union would go to pieces in a twelvemonth. But contact with all parts of the country brings understanding, rubs the edge off prejudice, promotes a candid consideration of the position of others. Prejudiced or uninformed the American may sometimes be; wantonly unjust—I say it deliberately—never. Another good result, as I take it, of the deification of business is that it keeps democracy fresh and wholesome. Commerce is the most democratic of all pursuits. In the august presence of the dollar all men are equal. It is not this man who graduated at Harvard against that man who herded swine; it is this man's credit and capital as set down in 'Bradstreet'—an amiable little work which gives the money value of every business man in the States, and computes the degree of trust that may be reposed in his signed paper—as against that other man's.

But all this is hideously materialistic. No doubt: only what do you mean by materialistic? In a sense, which I will explain in a page or two, the Americans appear to me the most materialistic people in the world. But as for the love of money, I don't think they are down with it any worse than any other people. I still think, as I said at the very beginning, that it is not the dollars they worship but the faculties that got them. The man who has made money in this country has attained what is the one aim of ninety-nine out of every hundred of his countrymen. He has had the ability to do what everybody is trying to do. Is it wonderful that he is respected? It would be wonderful indeed if he were not.

Cut off from the hard-won civilisation of the Old World, and left to struggle by themselves with the forest and the prairie, it was inevitable that the Americans should prize most highly those less highly-organised qualities of the mind which insured success in the struggle. The others may come with time. In the meanwhile there is the consolation for those who go down. Failure may be complete, but it is never irredeemable. In Europe a boy goes into a bank; he may hate it, but in the bank he usually remains. In America he will next appear in a newspaper office, then behind a draper's counter, then in Congress, then in bankruptcy, and then in a gold-mine. You never meet the man who has got a good place and don't mean to lose it. No place is good enough for the American's estimate of his own deserts—nor is the estimate inexcusable, for no possibility is beyond his legitimate aspiration. Nobody is ever done with. And this applies to the millionaire as well as to the starveling. A man of huge fortune is always breaking out, like Mr. Armour, into some new and unfamiliar trade. I have met a gentleman who made a large fortune as an ironmaster. One day it occurred to him to buy a newspaper. He did not know small pica from nonpareil, and by the time he was mastering the difference his fortune had melted away, and he had a mortgage on the house his wife and children lived in. He went about his business with an unmoved face. Why not? This was his life. He was playing the great game for the pleasure of playing it; and he played it and won it like a man.

Perhaps the most insightful analysis of the American mania for hard work was given by Hugo Münsterberg. Born and educated in Germany, Münsterberg came to the United States in 1892 to accept an appointment as professor of psychology at Harvard University. In The Americans *(Boston and New York, 1904), pp. 235-39, he brought his psychological training to bear on the phenomenon of working Americans.*

It always strikes the European as remarkable how very industrious American society is, and how relatively little bent on pleasure. It has often been said that the American has not yet learned how to enjoy life; that he knows very well how to make money, but not how to enjoy it. And that is quite true; except that it leaves out of account the main point—which is, that the American takes the keenest delight in the employment of all his faculties in his work, and in the exercise of his own initiative. This gives him more pleasure than the spending of money could bring him.

It is, therefore, fundamentally false to stigmatize the American as a materialist, and to deny his idealism. . . . The economic life means to the American a realizing of efforts which are in themselves precious. It is not the means to an end, but is its own end. If two blades of grass grow where one grew before, or two railroad tracks where there was but one; if production, exchange, and commerce increase and undertaking thrives, then life is created, and this is, in itself, a precious thing. The European of the Continent esteems the industrial life as honest, but not as noble; economic activities seem to him good for supporting himself and his family, but his duty is merely to supply economic needs which are now existing.

The merchant in Europe does not feel himself to be a free creator like the artist or scholar: his is no discoverer, no maker; and the mental energy which he expends he feels to be spent in serving an inferior purpose, which he serves only because he has to live. That creating economic values can itself by the very highest sort of accomplishment, and in itself alone desirable, whether or not it is useful for the person who creates, and that it is great in itself to spread and increase the life of the national economic organization, has been, indeed, felt by many great merchants in the history of Europe, and many a Hanseatic leader realizes it today. But the whole body of people in Europe does not know this, while America is thoroughly filled with the idea. . . . Every individual feels himself exalted by being a part of such a mighty whole, and the general intellectual effects of this temper show themselves in the entire national life.

A nation can never do its best in any direction unless it believes thoroughly in the intrinsic value of its work; whatever is done merely through necessity is never of great national significance, and second-rate men never achieve the highest things. If the first minds of a nation look down with contempt on economic life, if there is no real belief in the ideal value of industry, and if creative minds hold aloof from it, that nation will necessarily be outdone by others in the economic field. But where the ablest strength engages with idealistic enthusiasm in the service of the national economic problems, the nation rewards what the people do as done in the name of civilization, and the love of fame and work together spur them on more than the material gain which they will get. Indeed, this gain is itself only their measure of success in the service of civilization.

The American merchant works for money in exactly the sense that a great painter works for money; the high price which is paid for his picture is a very welcome indication of the general appreciation of his art: but he would never get this appreciation if he were working for the money instead of his artistic ideals. Economically to open up this gigantic country, to bring the fields and forests, rivers and mountains into the service of economic progress, to incite the millions of inhabitants to have new needs and to satsify these by their own resourcefulness, to increase the wealth of the nation, and finally economically to rule the world and within the nation itself to raise the economic power of the individual to undreamt-of importance, has been the work which has fascinated the American. And every individual has felt his co-operation to be ennobled by his firm belief in the value of such an aim for the culture of the world.

To find one's self in the service of this work of progress attracts even the small boy. As a German boy commences early to write verses or draw little sketches, in America the young farmer lad or city urchin tries to come somehow into this national, industrial activity; and whether he sells newspapers on the street or milks the cow on a neighbour's farm, he is proud of the few cents which he brings home—not because it is money, but because he has earned it, and the coins are the only possible proof that his activities have contributed to the economic life of his country. It is this alone which spurs him on and fills him with ambition; and if the young newspaper boy becomes a great railroad president, or the farmer's lad a wealthy factory owner, and both, although worth their millions, still work on from morning till night consumed by the thought of adding to the economic life of their nation, and to this end undertake all sorts of new enterprises, the labour itself has been, from beginning to end, its own reward. The content of such a man's life is the work of economic progress.

Men who have so felt have made the nation great, and no American would admit that a man who gave his life to government or to law, to art or science, would be able to make his life at all more significant or valuable for the ends of culture. This is not materialism. Thus it happens that the most favoured youths, the socially most competent talents, go into economic life, and the sons of the best families, after their course at the university, step enthusiastically into the business house. One can see merely from ordinary conversation how thoroughly the value of economic usefulness is impressed on the people. They speak in America of industrial movements with as much general interest as one would find manifested in Europe over politics, science, or art. Men who do not themselves anticipate buying or selling securities in the stock market, nevertheless discuss the rise and fall of various industrial and railroad shares as they would discuss Congressional debates; and any new industrial undertaking in a given city fills the citizens with pride, as may be gathered from their chance conversations.

The central point of this whole activity is, therefore, not greed, nor the thought of money, but the spirit of self-initiative. It is not surprising that this has gone through such a lively development. Just as the spirit of self-determination was the product of Colonial days, so the spirit of self-initiative is the necessary outcome of pioneer life.

VI. BLACK AND RED AMERICANS

In contrast to those aggressive, property-owning Americans who were exhausting themselves in the hectic rush toward success and wealth, Negroes and Indians were exploited and suppressed in nineteenth-century America. How did foreign visitors compare them with white Americans? What did their comments reveal about their attitudes toward non-white people? Why did the Negroes and Indians appear to be lazy? Why were they in such a subservient state? What hope did they have of achieving some measure of dignity and freedom? What was the "Indian problem"? Who created it? Which group appeared more destitute and deprived? In what terms did the visitors envisage the future of each group? How accurate were their predictions?

One could not go into the South during the first half of the nineteenth century without observing the condition of the Negro slaves. In 1832 Frances Kemble, a young English actress, accompanied her father on a visit to the United States. In Philadelphia she met Pierce Butler, a southern plantation owner, married him in 1834, and went to live on his two large estates near Darien, Georgia. Shocked at the predicament of the slaves under her husband's control, she soon began recording her impressions. The following notes, from The Journal of a Residence on a Georgian Plantation in 1838-1839 *(New York, 1863), pp. 87-89, 121-22, 174-75, were set in the form of letters to a friend, Elizabeth Dwight Sedgwick, in Massachusetts.*

A very curious and interesting circumstance to me just now in the neighborhood is the projection of a canal, to be called the Brunswick Canal, which, by cutting through the lower part of the main land, toward the southern extremity of Great St. Simon's Island, is contemplated as a probable and powerful means of improving the prosperity of the town of Brunswick, by bringing it into immediate communication with the Atlantic. The scheme, which I think I have mentioned to you before, is, I believe, chiefly patronized by your States' folk —Yankee enterprise and funds being very essential elements, it appears to me, in all Southern projects and achievements. This speculation, however, from all I hear of the difficulties of the undertaking, from the nature of the soil, and the impossibility almost of obtaining efficient labor, is not very likely to arrive at any very satisfactory result; and, very likely to arrive at any very satisfactory result; and, indeed, I find it hard to conceive how this part of Georgia can possibly produce a town which can be worth the digging of a canal, even to Yankee speculators. There is one feature of the undertaking, however, which more than all the others excites my admiration, namely, that Irish laborers have been advertised for to work upon the canal, and the terms offered them are twenty dollars a month per man and their board. Now these men will have for fellow-laborers negroes who not only will receive nothing at all for their work, but who will be hired by the contractors and directors of the works from their masters, to whom they will hand over the price of their slaves' labor; while it will be the interest of the person hiring them not only to get as much work as possible out of them, but also to provide them as economically with food, combining the two praiseworthy endeavors exactly in such judicious proportions as not to let them neutralize each other. You will observe that this case of a master hiring out his slaves to another employer, from whom he receives their rightful wages, is a form of slavery which, though extremely common, is very seldom adverted to in those arguments for the system which are chiefly founded upon the master's presumed regard for his human property. People who have ever let a favorite house to the temporary occupation of strangers can form a tolerable idea of the difference between one's own regard and care of one's goods and chattels and that of the most conscientious tenant; and whereas I have not yet observed that ownership is a very effectual protection to the slaves against ill usage and neglect, I am quite prepared to admit that it is a vastly better one than the temporary interest which a lessee can feel in the live-stock he hires, out of whom it is his manifest interest to get as much, and into whom to put as little, as possible. Yet thousands of slaves throughout the Southern states are thus handed over by the masters who own them to masters who do not; and it does not require much demonstration to prove that their estate is not always the more gracious. Now you must not suppose that these same Irish free laborers and negro slaves will be permitted to work together at this Brunswick Canal. They say that this would be utterly impossible; for why? there would be tumults, and risings, and broken heads, and bloody bones, and all the natural results of Irish intercommunion with their fellow-creatures, no doubt—perhaps even a little more riot and violence than merely comports with their usual habits of Milesian good fellowship; for, say the masters, the Irish hate the negroes more even than the Americans do, and there would be no bound to their murderous animosity if they were brought in contact with them on the same portion of the works of the Brunswick Canal. Doubtless there is some truth in this; the Irish laborers who might come hither would be apt enough, according to a universal moral law, to visit upon others the injuries they had received from others. They have been oppressed enough themselves to be oppressive whenever they have a chance; and the despised and degraded condition of the blacks, presenting to them a very ugly resemblance of their own home, circumstances naturally excite in them the exercise of the disgust and contempt of which they themselves are very habitually the objects; and that such circular distribution of wrongs may not only be pleasant, but have something like the air of retributive right to very ignorant folks, is not much to be wondered at. Certain is the fact, however, that the worst of all tyrants is the one who has been a slave; and, for that matter (and I wonder if the Southern slaveholders hear it with the same ear that I do, and ponder it with the same mind?), the command of one slave to another is altogether the most uncompromising utterance of insolent truculent despotism that it ever fell to my lot to witness or listen to. "You nigger—I say, you black nigger—you no hear me call you—what for you no run quick?" All this, dear E——, is certainly reasonably in favor of division of labor on the Brunswick Canal . . .

On my return to our own island I visited another of the hospitals, and the settlements to which it belonged. The condition of these places and of their inhabitants is, of course, the same all over the plantation, and if I were to describe them I should but weary you with a repetition of identical phenomena: filthy, wretched, almost naked, always barelegged and barefooted children; negligent, ignorant, wretched mothers, whose apparent indifference to the plight of their offspring, and utter incapacity to alter it, are the inevitable result of their slavery. It is hopeless to attempt to reform their habits or improve their condition while the women are condemned to field labor; nor is it possible to overestimate the bad moral effect of the system as regards the women entailing this enforced separation from their children, and neglect of all the cares and duties of mother, nurse, and even housewife, which are all merged in the mere physical toil of a human hoeing machine. It seems to me too—but upon this point I can not, of course, judge as well as the persons accustomed to and acquainted with the physical capacities of their slaves—that the labor is not judiciously distributed in many cases—at least not as far as the women are concerned. It is true that every able-bodied woman is made the most of in being driven afield as long as, under all and any circumstances, she is able to wield a hoe; but, on the other hand, stout, hale, hearty girls and boys, of from eight to twelve and older, are allowed to lounge about, filthy and idle, with no pretense of an occupation but what they call "tend baby," *i.e.*, see to the life and limbs of the little slave infants, to whose mothers, working in distant fields, they carry them during the day to be suckled, and for the rest of the time leave them to crawl and kick in the filthy cabins or on the broiling sand which surrounds them, in which industry, excellent enough for the poor babies, these big lazy youths and lasses emulate them. Again, I find many women who have borne from five to ten children rated as workers, precisely as young women in the prime of their strength who have had none; this seems a cruel carelessness. To be sure, while the women are pregnant their task is diminished, and this is one of the many indirect inducements held out to reckless propagation, which has a sort of premium offered to it in the consideration of less work and more food, counterbalanced by none of the sacred responsibilities which hallow and ennoble the relation of parent and child; in short, as their lives are for the most part those of mere animals, their increase is literally mere animal breeding, to which every encouragement is given, for it adds to the master's live-stock and the value of his estate. . . .

This morning I had a visit from two of the women, Charlotte and Judy, who came to me for help and advice for a complaint, which it really seems to me every other woman on the estate is cursed with, and which is a direct result of the conditions of their existence; the practice of sending women to labor in the fields in the third week after their confinement is a specific for causing this infirmity, and I know no specific for curing it under these circumstances. As soon as these poor things had departed with such comfort as I could give them, and the bandages they especially begged for, three other sable graces introduced themselves, Edie, Louisa, and Diana; the former told me she had had a family of seven children, but had lost them all through "ill luck," as she denominated the ignorance and ill treatment which were answerable for the loss of these, as of so many other poor little creatures their fellows. Having dismissed her and Diana with the sugar and rice they came to beg, I detained Louisa, whom I had never seen but in the presence of her old grandmother, whose version of the poor child's escape to, and hiding in the woods, I had a desire to compare with the heroine's own story. She told it very simply, and it was most pathetic. She had not finished her task one day, when she said she felt ill, and unable to do so, and had been severely flogged by Driver Bran, in whose "gang" she then was. The next day, in spite of this encouragement to labor, she had again been unable to complete her appointed work; and Bran having told her that he'd tie her up and flog her if she did not get it done, she had left the field and run into the swamp. "Tie you up, Louisa!" said I; "what is that?" She then described to me that they were fastened up by their wrists to a beam or a branch of a tree, their feet barely touching the ground, so as to allow them no purchase for resistance or evasion of the lash, their clothes turned over their heads, and their backs scored with a leather thong, either by the driver himself, or, if he pleases to inflict their punishment by deputy, any of the men he may choose to summon to the office; it might be father, brother, husband, or lover, if the overseer so ordered it. I turned sick, and my blood curdled listening to these details from the slender young slip of a lassie, with her poor piteous face and murmuring, pleading voice. "Oh," said I, "Louisa; but the rattlesnakes—the dreadful rattlesnakes in the swamps; were you not afraid of those horrible creatures?'' ''Oh, missis,'' said the poor child, ''me no tink of dem; me forget all 'bout dem for de fretting.'' ''Why did you come home at last?'' ''Oh, missis, me starve with hunger, me most dead with hunger before me come back.'' ''And were you flogged, Louisa?'' said I, with a shudder at what the answer might be. ''No, missis, me go to hospital; me almost dead and sick so long, 'spec Driver Bran him forgot 'bout de flogging.'' I am getting perfectly savage over all these doings, E——, and really think I should consider my own throat and those of my children well cut if some night the people were to take it into their heads to clear off scores in that fashion.

Some observers of Southern slavery were more dispassionate than Frances Kemble. Charles Lyell, a geologist from England, visited the United States in 1841 and again in 1845-46. In A Second Visit to the United States of North America *(2 vols.; London, 1850), vol. 1, pp. 276-79, 352-58, Lyell described the Negroes and slave conditions in Virginia and Georgia.*

Several Virginian planters have spoken to me of the negro race, as naturally warm-hearted, patient, and cheerful, grateful for benefits, and forgiving of injuries. They are also of a religious temperament bordering on superstition. Even those who think they ought for ever to remain in servitude give them a character which leads one to the belief that steps ought long ago to have been taken towards their gradual emancipation. Had some legislative provision been made with this view before the annexation of Texas, a period being fixed after which all the children born in this State should be free, that new territory would have afforded a useful outlet for the black population of Virginia, and whites would have supplied the vacancies which are now filled up by the breeding of negroes. In the absence of such enactments, Texas prolongs the duration of negro slavery in Virginia, aggravating one of its worst consequences, the internal slave trade, and keeping up the price of negroes at home. They are now selling for 500, 750, and 1000 dollars each, according to their qualifications. There are always dealers at Richmond, whose business it is to collect slaves for the southern market, and, until a gang is ready to start for the south, they are kept here well fed, and as cheerful as possible. In a court of the gaol, where they are lodged, I see them every day amusing themselves by playing at quoits. How much this traffic is abhorred, even by those who encourage it, is shown by the low social position held by the dealer, even when he has made a large fortune. When they conduct gangs of fifty slaves at a time across the mountains to the Ohio river, they usually manacle some of the men, but on reaching Ohio, they have no longer any fear of their attempting an escape, and they then unshackle them.

That the condition of slaves in Virginia is steadily improving, all here seem agreed. One of the greatest evils of the system is the compulsory separation of members of the same family. Since my arrival at Richmond, a case has come to my knowledge of a negro who petitioned a rich individual to purchase him, because he was going to be sold, and was in danger of being sent to New Orleans, his wife and child remaining in Virginia. But such instances are far less common than would be imagined, owing to the kind feeling of the southern planters towards their "own people," as they call them. Even in extreme cases, where the property of an insolvent is brought to the hammer, public opinion acts as a powerful check against the parting of kindred. We heard of two recent cases, one in which the parents were put up without their children, and the mother being in tears, no one would bid till the dealer put the children up also. They then sold very well. Another, where the dealer was compelled, in like manner, to sell a father and son together. I learnt with pleasure an anecdote, from undoubted authority, very characteristic of the indulgence of owners of the higher class of society here towards their slaves. One of the judges of the Supreme Court at Richmond having four or five supernumerary negroes in his establishment, proposed to them to go to his plantation in the country. As they had acquired town habits, they objected, and begged him instead to look out for a good master who would carry them to a city farther south, where they might enjoy a warm climate. The judge accordingly made his arrangements, and, for the sake of securing the desired conditions, was to receive for each a price below their market value. Just as they were about to leave Richmond for Louisiana, one of the women turned faint-hearted, at which all the rest lost courage; for their local and personal attachments are very strong, although they seem always ready to migrate cheerfully to any part of the world with their owners. The affair ended in the good-natured judge having to repurchase them, paying the difference of price between the sum agreed upon for each, and what they would have fetched at an auction.

Great sacrifices are often made from a sense of duty, by retaining possession of inherited estates, which it would be most desirable to sell, and which the owners cannot part with, because they feel it would be wrong to abandon the slaves to an unknown purchaser. We became acquainted with the family of a widow, who had six daughters and no son to take on himself the management of a plantation, always a responsible, and often a very difficult undertaking. It was felt by all the relatives and neighbours to be most desirable that the property, situated in a remote part of the country near the sea, should be sold, in order that the young ladies and their mother should have the benefit of society in a large town. They wished it themselves, being in very moderate circumstances, but were withheld by conscientious motives from leaving a large body of dependents, whom they had known from their childhood, and who could scarcely hope to be treated with the same indulgence by strangers. . . .

During a fortnight's stay at Hopeton, we had an opportunity of seeing how the planters live in the South, and the condition and prospects of the negroes on a well-managed estate. The relation of the slaves to their owners resembles nothing in the Northern States. There is an hereditary regard and often attachment on both sides, more like that formerly existing between lords and their retainers in the old feudal times of Europe, than to any thing now to be found in America. The slaves identify themselves with the master, and their sense of their own importance rises with his success in life. But the responsibility of the owners is felt to be great, and to manage a plantation with profit is no easy task, so much judgment is required, and such a mixture of firmness, forbearance, and kindness. The evils of the system of slavery are said to be exhibited in their worst light when new settlers come from the Free States; northern men, who are full of activity, and who strive to make a rapid fortune, willing to risk their own lives in an unhealthy climate, and who cannot make allowance for the repugnance to continuous labour of the negro race, or the diminished motive for exertion of the slave. To one who arrives in Georgia direct from Europe, with a vivid impression on his mind of the state of the peasantry there in many populous regions, their ignorance, intemperance, and improvidence, the difficulty of obtaining subsistence, and the small chance they have of bettering their lot, the condition of the black labourers on such a property as Hopeton, will afford but small ground for lamentation or despondency. I had many opportunities while here of talking with the slaves alone, or seeing them at work. I may be told that this was a favourable specimen of a well-managed estate; if so, I may at least affirm that mere chance led me to pay this visit, that is to say, scientific objects wholly unconnected with the "domestic institutions" of the South, or the character of the owner in relation to his slaves; and I may say the same in regard to every other locality or proprietor visited by me in the course of this tour. I can but relate what passed under my own eyes, or what I learnt from good authority, concealing nothing. . . .

The out-door labourers have separate houses provided for them; even the domestic servants, except a few who are nurses to the white children, live apart from the great house—an arrangement not always convenient for the masters, as there is no one to answer a bell after a certain hour. But if we place ourselves in the condition of the majority of the population—that of servants—we see at once how many advantages we should enjoy over the white race in the same rank of life in Europe. In the first place all can marry; and if a mistress should lay on any young woman here the injunction so common in English newspaper advertisements for a maid of all-work, "no followers allowed," it would be considered an extraordinary act of tyranny. The labourers begin work at six o'clock in the morning, have an hour's rest at nine for breakfast, and many have finished their assigned task by two o'clock, all of them by three o'clock. In summer they divide their work differently, going to bed in the middle of the day, then rising to finish their task, and afterwards spending a great part of the night in chatting, merry-making, preaching, and psalm-singing. At Christmas they claim a week's holidays, when they hold a kind of Saturnalia, and the owners can get no work done. Although there is scarcely any drinking, the master rejoices when this season is well over without mischief. The negro houses are as neat as the greater part of the cottages in Scotland (no flattering compliment it must be confessed), are provided always with a back door, and a hall, as they call it, in which is a chest, a table, two or three chairs, and a few shelves for crockery. . . .

One day, when walking alone, I came upon a "gang" of negroes, who were digging a trench. They were superintended by a black "driver," who held up a whip in his hand. Some of the labourers were using spades, others cutting away the roots and stumps of trees which they had encountered in the line of the ditch. Their mode of proceeding in their task was somewhat leisurely, and eight hours a day of this work are exacted, though they can accomplish the same in five hours, if they undertake it by the task. The digging of a given number of feet in length, breadth, and depth is, in this case, assigned to each ditcher, and a deduction made when they fall in with the stump or root. The names of gangs and drivers are odious, and the sight of the whip was painful to me as a mark of degradation, reminding me that the lower orders of slaves are kept to their work by mere bodily fear, and that treatment must depend on the individual character of the owner or overseer. That the whip is rarely used, and often held for weeks over them, merely *in terrorem,* is, I have no doubt, true on all well-governed estates; and it is not that formidable weapon which I have seen exhibited as formerly in use in the West Indies. It is a thong of leather, half an inch wide and a quarter of an inch thick. No ordinary driver is allowed to give more than six lashes for any offence, the head driver twelve, and the overseer twenty-four. When an estate is under superior management, the system is remarkably effective in preventing crime. The most severe punishment required in the last forty years for a body of 500 negroes at Hopeton was for the theft of one negro from another. In that period there has been no criminal act of the highest grade, for which a delinquent could be committed to the Penitentiary in Georgia, and there have been only six cases of assault and battery. As a race, the negroes are mild and forgiving, and by no means so prone to indulge in drinking as the white man or the Indian. There were more serious quarrels, and more broken heads, among the Irish in a few years, when they came to dig the Brunswick Canal, than had been known among the negroes in all the surrounding plantations for half a century.

*When most European visitors looked at the Negro and the Indian,
they saw two separate problems. Alexis de Tocqueville characteristi-
cally saw only one. The following excerpts are taken from* Democracy
in America, *translated by Henry Reeve, (London, 1862), vol. 1, pp.
393-399, 405-409, 412-423.*

The principal part of the task which I had imposed upon myself
is now performed: I have shown, as far as I was able, the laws and
the manners of the American democracy. Here I might stop; but the
reader would perhaps feel that I had not satisfied his expectations.

The absolute supremacy of democracy is not all that we meet with
in America; the inhabitants of the New World may be considered from
more than one point of view. In the course of this work my subject
has often led me to speak of the Indians and the Negroes; but I have
never been able to stop in order to show what place these two races
occupy, in the midst of the democratic people whom I was engaged
in describing. I have mentioned in what spirit, and according to what
laws, the Anglo-American Union was formed; but I could only glance
at the dangers which meance that confederation, whilst it was equally
impossible for me to give a detailed account of its chances of duration,
independently of its laws and manners. When speaking of the United
republican States, I hazarded no conjectures upon the permanence of
republican forms in the New World, and when making frequent allu-
sion to the commercial activity which reigns in the Union, I was
unable to inquire into the future condition of the Americans as a commercial people.

These topics are collaterally connected with my subject without
forming a part of it; they are American without being democratic;
and to portray democracy has been my principal aim. It was therefore
necessary to postpone these questions, which I now take up as the
proper termination of my work.

The territory now occupied or claimed by the American Union
spreads from the shores of the Atlantic to those of the Pacific Ocean.
On the East and West its limits are those of the continent itself. On
the South it advances nearly to the Tropic, and it extends upwards
to the icy regions of the North.

The human beings who are scattered over this space do not form,

as in Europe, so many branches of the same stock. Three races, naturally distinct, and, I might almost say, hostile to each other, are dis-
coverable amongst them at the first glance. Almost insurmountable
barriers had been raised between them by education and by law, as
well as by their origin and outward characteristics; but fortune has
brought them together on the same soil, where, although they are
mixed, they do not amalgamate, and each race fulfills its destiny apart.

Amongst these widely differing families of men, the first which
attracts attention, the superior in intelligence, in power and in enjoyment, is the White or European, the MAN pre-eminent; and in subor-
dinate grades, the Negro and the Indian. These two unhappy races
have nothing in common; neither birth, nor features, nor language,
nor habits. Their only resemblance lies in their misfortunes. Both of
them occupy an inferior rank in the country they inhabit; both suffer
from tyranny; and if their wrongs are not the same, they originate,
at any rate, with the same authors.

If we reasoned from what passes in the world, we should almost
say that the European is to the other races of mankind, what man
is to the lower animals;—he makes them subservient to his use; and
when he cannot subdue, he destroys them. Oppression has, at one
stroke, deprived the descendants of the Africans of almost all the
privileges of humanity. The Negro of the United States has lost all
remembrance of his country; the language which his forefathers spoke
is never heard around him; he abjured their religion and forgot their
customs when he ceased to belong to Africa, without acquiring any
claim to European privileges. But he remains half-way between the
two communities; sold by the one, repulsed by the other; finding not
a spot in the universe to call by the name of country, except the faint
image of a home which the shelter of his master's roof affords.

The Negro has no family; woman is merely the temporary companion of his pleasures, and his children are upon an equality with himself
from the moment of their birth. Am I to call it a proof of God's
mercy or a visitation of his wrath, that man, in certain states, appears
to be insensible to his extreme wretchedness, and almost affects, with
a depraved taste, the cause of his misfortunes? The Negro, who is
plunged in this abyss of evils, scarcely feels his own calamitous situation. Violence made him a slave, and the habit of servitude gives
him the thoughts and desires of a slave; he admires his tyrants more

than he hates them, and finds his joy and his pride in the servile imita-
tion of those who oppress him: his understanding is degraded to the
level of his soul.

The Negro enters upon slavery as soon as he is born; nay, he may
have been purchased in the womb, and have begun his slavery before
he began his existence. Equally devoid of wants and of enjoyment,
and useless to himself, he learns, with his first notions of existence,
that he is the property of another who has an interest in preserving
his life, and that the care of it does not devolve upon himself; even
the power of thought appears to him a useless gift of Providence,
and he quietly enjoys the privileges of his debasement.

If he becomes free, independence is often felt by him to be a heavier
burden than slavery; for having learned, in the course of his life, to
submit to everything except reason, he is too much unacquainted with
her dictates to obey them. A thousand new desires beset him, and
he is destitute of the knowledge and energy necessary to resist them:
these are masters which it is necessary to contend with, and he has
learnt only to submit and obey. In short, he sinks to such a depth
of wretchedness, that while servitude brutalizes, liberty destroys him.

Oppression has been no less fatal to the Indian than to the Negro
race, but its effects are different. Before the arrival of white men in
the New World, the inhabitants of North America lived quietly in their
woods, enduring the vicissitudes and practising the virtues and vices
common to savage nations. The Europeans, having dispersed the
Indian tribes and driven them into the deserts, condemned them to
a wandering life full of inexpressible sufferings.

Savage nations are only controlled by opinion and by custom. When
the North American Indians had lost the sentiment of attachment to
their country; when their families were dispersed, their traditions
obscured, and the chain of their recollections broken; when all their
habits were changed, and their wants increased beyond measure, European tyranny rendered them more disorderly and less civilized than
they were before. The moral and physical condition of these tribes
continually grew worse, and they became more barbarous as they
became more wretched. Nevertheless, the Europeans have not been
able to metamorphose the character of the Indians; and though they
have had power to destroy them, they have never been able to make
them submit to the rules of civilized society.

The lot of the Negro is placed on the extreme limit of servitude, while that of the Indian lies on the uttermost verge of liberty; and slavery does not produce more fatal effects upon the first, than independence upon the second. The Negro has lost all property in his own person, and he cannot dispose of his existence without committing a sort of fraud: but the savage is his own master as soon as he is able to act; parental authority is scarcely known to him; he has never bent his will to that of any of his kind, nor learned the difference between voluntary obedience and a shameful subjection; and the very name of law is unknown to him. To be free, with him, signifies to escape from all the shackles of society. As he delights in this barbarous independence, and would rather perish than sacrifice the least part of it, civilization has little power over him.

The Negro makes a thousand fruitless efforts to insinuate himself amongst men who repulse him; he conforms to the tastes of his oppressors, adopts their opinions, and hopes by imitating them to form a part of their community. Having been told from infancy that his race is naturally inferior to that of the Whites, he assents to the proposition, and is ashamed of his own nature. In each of his features he discovers a trace of slavery, and, if it were in his power, he would willingly rid himself of everything that makes him what he is.

The Indian, on the contrary, has his imagination inflated with the pretended nobility of his origin, and lives and dies in the midst of these dreams of pride. Far from desiring to conform his habits to ours, he loves his savage life as the distinguishing mark of his race, and he repels every advance to civilization, less perhaps from the hatred which he entertains for it, than from a dread of resembling the Europeans. While he has nothing to oppose to our perfection in the arts but the resources of the desert, to our tactics nothing but undisciplined courage; whilst our well-digested plans are met by the spontaneous instincts of savage life, who can wonder if he fails in this unequal contest?

The Negro, who earnestly desires to mingle his race with that of the European, cannot effect it; while the Indian, who might succeed to a certain extent, disdains to make the attempt. The servility of the one dooms him to slavery, the pride of the other to death.

I remember that while I was travelling through the forests which still cover the State of Alabama, I arrived one day at the log-house of a pioneer. I did not wish to penetrate into the dwelling of the American, but retired to rest myself for a while on the margin of a spring, which was not far off, in the woods. While I was in this place, (which was in the neighbourhood of the Creek territory,) an Indian woman appeared, followed by a Negress, and holding by the hand a little white girl of five or six years old, whom I took to be the daughter of the pioneer. A sort of barbarous luxury set off the costume of the Indian; rings of metal were hanging from her nostrils and ears; her hair, which was adorned with glass beads, fell loosely upon her shoulders; and I saw that she was not married, for she still wore that necklace of shells which the bride always deposits on the nuptial couch. The Negress was clad in squalid European garments.

They all three came and seated themselves upon the banks of the fountain; and the young Indian, taking the child in her arms, lavished upon her such fond caresses as mothers give; while the Negress endeavoured by various little artifices to attract the attention of the young Creole.

The child displayed in her slightest gestures a consciousness of superiority which formed a strange contrast with her infantine weakness; as if she received the attentions of her companions with a sort of condescension.

The Negress was seated on the ground before her mistress, watching her smallest desires, and apparently divided between strong affection for the child, and servile fear; whilst the savage displayed, in the midst of her tenderness, an air of freedom and of pride which was almost ferocious. I had approached the group, and I contemplated them in silence; but my curiosity was probably displeasing to the Indian woman, for she suddenly rose, pushed the child roughly from her, and giving me an angry look plunged into the thicket.

I had often chanced to see individuals met together in the same place, who belonged to the three races of men which people North America. I had perceived from many different results the preponderance of the Whites. But in the picture which I have just been describing there was something peculiarly touching; a bond of affection here united the oppressors with the oppressed, and the effort of Nature to bring them together rendered still more striking the immense distance placed between them by prejudice and by law.

The ejectment of the Indians very often takes place at the present day, in a regular, and, as it were, a legal manner. When the European population begins to approach the limit of the desert inhabited by a savage tribe, the Government of the United States usually dispatches envoys to them, who assemble the Indians in a large plain, and having first eaten and drunk with them, accost them in the following manner: "What have you to do in the land of your fathers? Before long, you must dig up their bones in order to live. In what respect is the country you inhabit better than another? Are there no woods, marshes, or prairies, except where you dwell? And can you live nowhere but under your own sun? Beyond those mountains which you see at the horizon, beyond the lake which bounds your territory on the West, there lie vast countries where beasts of chase are found in great abundance; sell your lands to us, and go to live happily in those solitudes." After holding this language, they spread before the eyes of the Indians fire-arms, woollen garments, kegs of brandy, glass necklaces, bracelets of tinsel, ear-rings, and looking-glasses. If, when they have beheld all these riches, they still hesitate, it is insinuated that they have not the means of refusing their required consent, and that the Government itself will not long have the power of protecting them in their rights. What are they to do? Half convinced, and half compelled, they go to inhabit new deserts, where the importunate Whites will not let them remain ten years in tranquillity. In this manner do the Americans obtain, at a very low price, whole provinces, which the richest sovereigns of Europe could not purchase.

These are great evils; and it must be added that they appear to me to be irremediable. I believe that the Indian nations of North America are doomed to perish; and that whenever the Europeans shall be established on the shores of the Pacific Ocean, that race of men will be no more. The Indians had only the two alternatives of war or civilization; in other words, they must either have destroyed the Europeans or become their equals.

At first settlement of the colonies they might have found it possible, by uniting their forces, to deliver themselves from the small bodies of strangers who landed on their continent. They several times attempted to do it, and were on the point of succeeding; but the disproportion of their resources, at the present day, when compared with those of the Whites, is too great to allow such an enterprise to be thought of. Nevertheless, there do arise from time to time among the

Indians men of penetration, who foresee the final destiny which awaits the native population, and who exert themselves to unite all the tribes in common hostility to the Europeans; but their efforts are unavailing. Those tribes which are in the neighbourhood of the Whites, are too much weakened to offer an effectual resistance: whilst the others, giving way to that childish carelessness of the morrow which characterizes savage life, wait for the near approach of danger before they prepare to meet it: some are unable, the others are unwilling, to exert themselves.

It is easy to foresee that the Indians will never conform to civilization; or that it will be too late, whenever they may be inclined to make the experiment.

Civilization is the result of a long social process which takes place in the same spot, and is handed down from one generation to another, each one profiting by the experience of the last. Of all nations, those submit to civilization with the most difficulty, which habitually live by the chase. Pastoral tribes, indeed, often change their place of abode; but they follow a regular order in their migrations, and often return again to their old stations, whilst the dwelling of the hunter varies with that of the animals he pursues.

Several attempts have been made to diffuse knowledge amongst the Indians, without controlling their wandering propensities; by the Jesuits in Canada, and by the Puritans in New England; but none of these endeavours were crowned by any lasting success. Civilization began in the cabin, but it soon retired to expire in the woods. The great error of these legislators of the Indians was their not understanding, that in order to succeed in civilizing a people, it is first necessary to fix it; which cannot be done without inducing it to cultivate the soil: the Indians ought in the first place to have been accustomed to agriculture. But not only are they destitute of this indispensable preliminary to civilization, they would even have great difficulty in acquiring it. Men who have once abandoned themselves to the restless and adventurous life of the hunter, feel an insurmountable disgust for the constant and regular labour which tillage requires. We see this proved in the bosom of our own society; but it is far more visible among peoples whose partiality for the chase is a part of their national character.

Independently of this general difficulty, there is another, which applies peculiarly to the Indians; they consider labour not merely as an evil, but as a disgrace; so that their pride prevents them from becoming civilized, as much as their indolence.

There is no Indian so wretched as not to retain under his hut of bark, a lofty idea of his personal worth; he considers the cares of industry and labour as degrading occupations; he compares the husbandman to the ox which traces the furrow; and even in our most ingenious handicraft, he can see nothing but the labour of slaves. Not that he is devoid of admiration for the power and intellectual greatness of the Whites; but although the result of our efforts surprises him, he contemns the means by which we obtain it; and while he acknowledges our ascendency, he still believes in his superiority. War and hunting are the only pursuits which appear to him worthy to be the occupations of a man. The Indian, in the dreary solitudes of his woods, cherishes the same ideas, the same opinions as the noble of the Middle Ages in his castle, and he only requires to become a conqueror to complete the resemblance: thus, however strange it may seem, it is in the forests of the New World, and not amongst the Europeans who people its coasts, that the ancient prejudices of Europe are still in existence.

If the Indian tribes which now inhabit the heart of the continent could summon up energy enough to attempt to civilize themselves, they might possibly succeed. Superior already to the barbarous nations which surround them, they would gradually gain strength and experience, and when the Europeans should appear upon their borders, they would be in a state, if not to maintain their independence, at least to assert their right to the soil, and to incorporate themselves with the conquerors. But it is the misfortune of Indians to be brought into contact with a civilized people, which is also (it must be owned) the most avaricious nation on the globe, whilst they are still semi-barbarian: to find despots in their instructors, and to receive knowledge from the hand of oppression. Living in the freedom of the woods, the North American Indian was destitute, but he had no feeling of inferiority towards any one; as soon, however, as he desires to penetrate into the social scale of the Whites, he takes the lowest rank in society, for he enters, ignorant and poor, within the pale of science and wealth. After having led a life of agitation, beset with evils and dangers, but at the same time filled with proud emotions, he is obliged to submit to a wearisome, obscure, and degraded state; and to gain the bread which nourishes him by hard and ignoble labour, such are in his eyes the only results of which civilization can boast: and even this much he is not sure to obtain.

When the Indians undertake to imitate their European neighbours, and to till the earth like the settlers, they are immediately exposed to a very formidable competition. The white man is skilled in the craft of agriculture; the Indian is a rough beginner in an art with which he is unacquainted. The former reaps abundant crops without difficulty, the latter meets with a thousand obstacles in raising the fruits of the earth.

The European is placed amongst a population whose wants he knows and partakes. The savage is isolated in the midst of a hostile people, with whose manners, language, and laws he is imperfectly acquainted, but without whose assistance he cannot live. He can only procure the materials of comfort by bartering his commodities against the goods of the European, for the assistance of his countrymen is wholly insufficient to supply his wants. When the Indian wishes to sell the produce of his labour, he cannot always meet with a purchaser, whilst the European readily finds a market; and the former can only produce at a considerable cost, that which the latter vends at a very low rate. Thus the Indian has no sooner escaped those evils to which barbarous nations are exposed, than he is subjected to the still greater miseries of civilized communities; and he finds it scarcely less difficult to live in the midst of our abundance, than in the depth of his own wilderness.

He has not yet lost the habits of his erratic life; the traditions of his fathers and his passion for the chase are still alive within him. The wild enjoyments which formerly animated him in the woods, painfully excite his troubled imagination; and his former privations appear to be less keen, his former perils less appalling. He contrasts the independence which he possessed amongst his equals with the servile position which he occupies in civilized society. On the other hand, the solitudes which were so long his free home are still at hand; a few hours' march will bring him back to them once more. The Whites offer him a sum, which seems to him to be considerable, for the ground which he has begun to clear. This money of the Europeans may possibly furnish him with the means of a happy and peaceful subsistence in remoter regions; and he quits the plough, resumes his native arms, and returns to the wilderness for ever. The condition of the Creeks and Cherokees, to which I have already alluded, sufficiently corroborates the truth of this deplorable picture.

The Indians, in the little which they have done, have unquestionably displayed as much natural genius as the peoples of Europe in their most important designs; but nations as well as men require time to learn, whatever may be their intelligence and their zeal. Whilst the savages were engaged in the work of civilization, the Europeans continued to surround them on every side, and to confine them within narrower limits; the two races gradually met, and they are now in immediate juxtaposition to each other. The Indian is already superior to his barbarous parent, but he is still very far below his white neighbour. With their resources and acquired knowledge, the Europeans soon appropriated to themselves most of the advantages which the natives might have derived from the possession of the soil: they have settled in the country, they have purchased land at a very low rate or have occupied it by force, and the Indians have been ruined by a competition which they had not the means of resisting. They were isolated in their own country, and their race only constituted a colony of troublesome aliens in the midst of a numerous and domineering people.

Washington said in one of his messages to Congress, ''We are more enlightened and more powerful than the Indian nations, we are therefore bound in honour to treat them with kindness and even with generosity.'' But this virtuous and high-minded policy has not been followed. The rapacity of the settlers is usually backed by the tyranny of the Government. Although the Cherokees and the Creeks are established upon the territory which they inhabited before the settlement of the Europeans, and although the Americans have frequently treated with them as with foreign nations, the surrounding States have not consented to acknowledge them as independent peoples, and attempts have been made to subject these children of the woods to Anglo-American magistrates, laws, and customs. Destitution had driven these unfortunate Indians to civilization, and oppression now drives them back to their former condition: many of them abandon the soil which they had begun to clear, and return to their savage course of life.

If we consider the tyrannical measures which have been adopted by the legislatures of the Southern States, the conduct of their Governors, and the decrees of their courts of justice, we shall be convinced that the entire expulsion of the Indians is the final result to which the efforts of their policy are directed. The Americans of that part of the Union look with jealousy upon the aborigines, they are aware that these tribes have not yet lost the traditions of savage life, and before civilization has permanently fixed them to the soil, it is intended to force them to recede by reducing them to despair. The Creeks and Cherokees, oppressed by the several States, have appealed to the central Government, which is by no means insensible to their misfortunes, and is sincerely desirous of saving remnant of the natives, and of maintaining them in the free possession of that territory, which the Union is pledged to respect. But the several States oppose so formidable a resistance to the execution of this design, that the Government is obliged to consent to the extirpation of a few barbarous tribes in order not to endanger the safety of the American Union.

But the Federal Government, which is not able to protect the Indians, would fain mitigate the hardships of their lot; and, with this intention, proposals have been made to transport them into more remote regions at the public cost.

Between the 33rd and 37th degrees of north latitude, a vast tract of country lies, which has taken the name of Arkansas, from the principal river that waters its extent. It is bounded on the one side by the confines of Mexico, on the other by the Mississippi. Numberless streams cross it in every direction; the climate is mild, and the soil productive, but it is only inhabited by a few wandering hordes of savages. The Government of the Union wishes to transport the broken remnants of the indigenous population of the South, to the portion of this country which is nearest to Mexico, and at a great distance from the American settlements.

We were assured, towards the end of the year 1831, that 10,000 Indians had already gone down to the shores of the Arkansas; and fresh detachments were constantly following them: but Congress has been unable to excite a unanimous determination in those whom it is disposed to protect. Some, indeed, are willing to quit the seat of oppression, but the most enlightened members of the community refuse to abandon their recent dwellings and their springing crops; they are of opinion that the work of civilization, once interrupted, will never be resumed; they fear that those domestic habits which have been so recently contracted, may be irrevocably lost in the midst of a country which is still barbarous, and where nothing is prepared for the subsistence of an agricultural people; they know that their entrance into those wilds will be opposed by inimical hordes, and that they have lost the energy of barbarians, without acquiring the resources of civilization to resist their attacks. Moreover, the Indians readily discover that the settlement which is proposed to them is merely a temporary expedient. Who can assure them that they will at length be allowed to dwell in peace in their new retreat? The United States pledge themselves to the observance of the obligation; but the territory which they at present occupy was formerly secured to them by the most solemn oaths of Anglo-American faith. The American Government does not indeed rob them of their lands, but it allows perpetual incursions to be made on them. In a few years the same white population which now flocks around them, will track them to the solitudes of the Arkansas; they will then be exposed to the same evils without the same remedies; and as the limits of the earth will at last fail them, their only refuge is the grave.

The Union treats the Indians with less cupidity and rigour than the policy of the several States, but the two Governments are alike destitute of good faith. The States extend what they are pleased to term the benefits of their laws to the Indians, with a belief that the tribes will recede rather than submit; and the central Government, which promises a permanent refuge to these unhappy beings, is well aware of its inability to secure it to them.

Thus the tyranny of the States obliges the savages to retire, the Union, by its promises and resources, facilitates their retreat; and these measures tend to precisely the same end. "By the will of our Father in Heaven, the Governor of the whole world," said the Cherokees in their petition to Congress, "the red man of America has become small, and the white man great and renowned. When the ancestors of the people of these United States first came to the shores of America, they found the red man strong; though he was ignorant and savage, yet he received them kindly, and gave them dry land to rest their weary feet. They met in peace, and shook hands in token of friendship. Whatever the white man wanted and asked of the Indian, the latter willingly gave. At that time the Indian was the lord, and the white man the suppliant. But now the scene has changed. The strength of the red man has become weakness. As his neighbours increased in numbers, his power became less and less, and now, of the many and powerful tribes who once covered these United States, only a few are to be seen—a few whom a sweeping pestilence has left. The northern tribes, who were once so numerous and powerful, are now nearly extinct. Thus it has happened to the red man of America. Shall we, who are remnants, share the same fate?

"The land on which we stand we have received as an inheritance from our fathers, who possessed it from time immemorial, as a gift from our common Father in Heaven. They bequeathed it to us as their children, and we have sacredly kept it, as containing the remains of our beloved men. This right of inheritance we have never ceded, nor ever forfeited. Permit us to ask what better right can the people have to a country than the right of inheritance and immemorial peaceable possession? We know it is said of late by the State of Georgia and by the Executive of the United States, that we have forfeited this right; but we think this is said gratuitously. At what time have we made the forfeit? What great crime have we committed, whereby we must for ever be divested of our country and rights? Was it when we were hostile to the United States, and took part with the King of Great Britain, during the struggle for Independence? If so, why was not this forfeiture declared in the first treaty of peace between the United States and our beloved men? Why was not such an article as the following inserted in the treaty: 'The United States give peace to the Cherokees, but, for the part they took in the late war, declare them to be but tenants at will, to be removed when the convenience of the States, within those chartered limits they live, shall require it'? That was the proper time to assume such a possession. But it was not thought of, nor would our forefathers have agreed to any treaty, whose tendency was to deprive them of their rights and their country."

Such is the language of the Indians: their assertions are true, their forebodings inevitable. From whichever side we consider the destinies of the aborigines of North America, their calamities appear to be irremediable: if they continue barbarous, they are forced to retire; if they attempt to civilize their manners, the contact of a more civilized community subjects them to oppression and destitution. They perish if they continue to wander from waste to waste, and if they attempt to settle, they still must perish; the assistance of Europeans is necessary to instruct them, but the approach of Europeans corrupts and repels them into savage life; they refuse to change their habits as long as their solitudes are their own, and it is too late to change them when they are constrained to submit.

The Spaniards pursued the Indians with blood-hounds, like wild beasts; they sacked the New World with no more temper or compassion than a city taken by storm: but destruction must cease, and frenzy be stayed; the remnant of the Indian population, which had escaped the massacre, mixed with its conquerors, and adopted in the end their religion and their manners. The conduct of the Americans of the United States towards the aborigines is characterized, on the other hand, by a singular attachment to the formalities of law. Provided that the Indians retain their barbarous condition, the Americans take no part in their affairs; they treat them as independent nations, and do not possess themselves of their hunting-grounds without a treaty of purchase: and if an Indian nation happens to be so encroached upon as to be unable to subsist upon its territory, they afford it brotherly assistance in transporting it to a grave sufficiently remote from the land of its fathers.

The Spaniards were unable to exterminate the Indian race by those unparalleled atrocities which brand them with indelible shame, nor did they even succeed in wholly depriving it of its rights; but the Americans of the United States have accomplished this twofold purpose with singular felicity; tranquilly, legally, philanthropically, without shedding blood, and without violating a single great principle of morality in the eyes of the world. It is impossible to destroy men with more respect for the laws of humanity.

The problems of the American Indian as well as those of the Negro attracted the attention of European visitors. One anonymous English settler reflected upon the treatment of Indians by whites in Hochelaga; or England in the New World, *ed. Eliot Warburton (2 vols.; London, 1851), vol. 2, pp. 301-7.*

The treatment of the Indian race in America, by the Europeans, has generally been contemptuous and cruel: the Spaniards were apparently the most unmerciful to them, but the inhabitants of the United States have been the most faithless. Since the union has become a nation, many treaties have been made with the Indians, but none respected; year after year, some great extent of territory is taken from them, and a paltry bribe given, instead, to the ignorant and corrupted chief. The people of the gentle and generous Pocahontas have perished from the land, and the magnanimous Mohicans are only remembered through the pages of a romance. The Indians who hover round the magnificent country of their fathers, now, the "land of the stranger," are few and scattered, weak and helpless, but the inextinguishable pride of their race upholds their spirit; they know that to resist the European is vain, but they despise him still, hate him and shun his civilization, although the manufactures and arms of the white men have become necessary to them. The animals of the chase recede constantly into the interior, they become fewer and more difficult of access; the only resource of the Indian is thus failing.

When the English settlers first landed in America, some of the tribes received them with kindness, others with a fierce hostility, but the fate of all was ultimately the same; as the mysterious prophecies of their old men declared, "a destruction came from the rising sun." Wherever the axe of the settler rings in the forest, the wild animals leave for far distant haunts, and the Indian must follow them. When the Americans have thus driven away the only supply of food, they call the Red Man to a meeting, and explain that this land is no longer useful for the chase, that the pale-faces will soon take it at any rate, while further away to the West there are boundless tracts ready to receive the Indians. At the same time are spread before them arms, clothing, and tinsel baubles, beads, and mirrors, to tempt them to the form of a sale; above all, the blinding and deadly fire-water decides the bargain. To obtain this poison, they will sacrifice lands and life itself. In this manner hundreds of thousands of acres have been purchased for a few thousand dollars; each sale accompanied by a treaty promising them protection in their remaining rights: but in a few years the attack is renewed, and so on, till none remain.

It seems to be ascertained that the Indian race cannot increase, or even exist, in contact with the Anglo-Saxon. Their ultimate fate must be, to wander off, a wretched remnant, to the dreary regions of the Hudson's Bay territory, till misery ends in death. But a very short time in the world's history will have cleared the buffalo and the deer from the South and central districts of America, by the spread of cultivation; their only refuge will be the North, and there will be found the last of the aboriginal men and beasts of the New World.

England has always been more strict in her dealings, and more considerate towards the Indians, than has America: the consequence is that her faith and credit stand much higher among them, and by the distant shores of the Great Western Lakes, the wandering Indian holds sacred the honour of an Englishman, as does the Egyptian in the streets of Cairo to this day. Many efforts have been made to civilize and save this doomed people; all have proved vain, for civilization cannot proceed without labour, and that they hate and regard as a degradation. There have been numberless instances of Indians being tolerably educated and accustomed to civilized life, but almost invariably they have returned to the freedom and hardships of the forest as soon as opportunity offered.

There are indeed settlements of the Cherokees and other tribes, which have exhibited some appearance of success and prosperity; but, every now and then, a sweep of disease thins their numbers, and, besides, their race mingles with the European blood, till they too melt away.

The great feature of the Indian character is pride. He considers war and the chase as the only occupations worthy of a man. Now, they have comparatively, but scanty grounds whereon to hunt and they are too weak for war, but still the pride remains indomitable—fatal. Even in the rare cases where they do make the effort to till the soil and enter upon a life of civilization, the sense of inferiority to the white man in these arts drives them to despair. Their unskilful hands and simple ignorance soon leave them in the very lowest grade of social condition. Most of the necessaries of life must be purchased from the white man; the scanty crops soon cease to supply the means; they become miserably poor, having contracted the wants of civilization without the power of satisfying them; their pride revolts at being thus bowed down before the strange race; and they either return to their life of savage freedom and hardship, or the firewater renders them insensible to their misery and degradation. The lands which even their imperfect toil has in some measure made valuable, are sold to supply present wants, and they go forth lost and outcast to the wilderness.

The few who struggle on against all these difficulties are looked upon but as troublesome aliens in the land; the white population surges round them on every side; year after year, the Indians decrease in number; portions of their land pass from their hands, till, at length, no trace remains to shew where they once dwelt.

In all these invasions and aggressions, the States have supported the white men, sometimes under the form of admitting the Indians to equality and receiving them as citizens, when of course they are instantly lost in the superiority of the European race. Many Americans do not scruple to assert in conversation that the final object of their system with regard to the Indians is their complete extirpation. The hard laws indeed allow them an alternative of wandering farther away to the West, into unknown tracts, or perishing miserably where they now are. The central government has tried several times humanely to interfere for their protection, but its feeble efforts proved useless where the interests of the separate States were concerned. An attempt was made to secure them a retreat in the distant territory of Arkansas, but already the spread of white population has reached these wilds, and extends to the confines of Mexico; while the poor Indian emigrant from the East had to struggle even there, with the fierce native tribes, who still retained the energy and courage of their savage state. When he obtained a footing, he had no encouragement to till the land, for he knew that even this was but a temporary residence.

Several times before, the American nation had given them solemn guarantees in treaties, that they should never be disturbed in the possession of the lands then theirs; but the turbulent and lawless settlers forced in everywhere among them and around them, till they could no longer remain. But now the tragedy is nearly over; few and feeble, weary and hopeless, up the far distant branches of the Arkansas they are hemmed in by the advancing tide of civilization on one side, by the jealous and hostile tribes of the interior on the other; and they now rapidly seek their only refuge, whither the white man must soon follow, not to oppress them more, but to render an account of his misdeeds—the refuge of the grave.

Another observer of the Indians was Henry Sienkiewicz, a Polish novelist who traveled in the United States in 1876-78. The following is from Charles Morley (ed. & tr.) Portrait of America: Letters of Henry Sienkiewicz, *New York: Columbia University Press, 1959, pp. 62-67, by permission of the publisher.*

It is difficult to comprehend the extent of the hatred and contempt of the American frontiersman for the Indian. It is true that a battle to the death was raging and that pillage and murder severely strain relations. But it is also true that the white frontiersmen do not regard the Indians as human beings and look upon their extermination as a service to humanity. According to the philosophy of the frontier, the white man has the same right to exterminate Indians as he would rattlesnakes, grizzly bears, and other harmful creatures. While New York curbstone philanthropists from time to time arrange charity balls at which Indians were exhibited, out on the frontier a merciless and dreadful war rages incessantly. One must understand that the frontiersmen, although loyal and even honest in their relations with each other, are no less savage than the redskins themselves when dealing with the latter. It is true that the Indian knows no mercy. A victim who falls into his hands would find all human prayer and pleading to no avail. The red warrior looks upon his victim with impassive eyes and supplications merely tickle his ears pleasantly. The suffering of his victim gives him pleasure, he feasts upon it, and for a while he is happy. And the whites treat the Indians in exactly the same manner. The Indian tears off the scalp of his captive as a war trophy; the whites have adopted this custom from the redskins and they likewise scalp their prisoners. In view of all this, if someone should ask me on whose side justice lies, I should answer that, judging in accordance with simple principles of justice, it lies on the side of the Indians.

Let us look at this vaunted civilization and see how it appears to the Indians who are declared incapable of adopting it. First of all, the government of the United States guarantees land to them, but the citizens from whose bosom the government sprang take the land from them in spite of the government. Thus, at the very outset, the Indian meets with deception and perjury and, as a simple child of nature, he is unable to differentiate between the government and the people. The Indian's sole impression from all this is that he has been deeply wronged. Moreover, the Indian sees in such a civilization only the destruction of everything which has served as a means of livelihood for him and his forefathers. First, the wide open prairies are taken from him and he is given a piece of land which he does not know how to cultivate. A horse blanket is given to him, but his liberty is taken from him. What an excellent exchange! The savage warrior astride the bare back of his mustang roams across the prairie. He hunts, fights, and fills his lungs with the fresh air. The wild, prairie life is as necessary to him as are the wide open heavens to the birds. Without it he cannot exist; he withers away and dies. Let us consider what he gains and what he loses by accepting so-called civilization. Above all, he suffers from hunger on his small piece of land. Those same "brothers" who preached to him of civilization, now look upon him with contempt, as we in Europe do upon the gypsies. Ultimately nothing remains for him but to lead the life of a gypsy: begging and thieving, living from hand to mouth, and steadily becoming more and more degraded.

Finally, who are these apostles of civilization with whom he comes in contact? First, there is the merchant who cheats him, then the adventurer who scalps him, next the trapper who hunts buffaloes right in front of his wigwam—the buffaloes that are the redskin's main source of livelihood, finally, the American government commissioner with his documents which contain, hidden between the lines, the motto *Mane, tekel, fares!* for the entire race.

Later at many of the railroad stations on the prairies of Nebraska and Wyoming, I met so-called civilized Indians. They present a uniform picture of misery and despair. The men are shabby, dirty, and degraded; the women stretch their emaciated hands toward the coaches, begging for handouts. You may inquire: why don't they work? They do not know how to work, and no one is concerned about teaching them. They have renounced their wars with the whites, and given up their raids and hunting. In return, they have received . . . horse blankets . . . and contempt.

Finally, the immediate benefits which all savages received as the direct result of civilization were whiskey, smallpox, and syphilis. Is it at all surprising, therefore, that upon viewing civilization from their experience of these first benefits, they do not yearn for it, but rather fight against it to the death?

Most of them perish. Entire tribes, whether they accept civilization or continue to lead a wild life, are vanishing from the face of the earth with frightening speed. They can neither resist civilization nor support its heavy burden upon their weak shoulders. . . . As for the Indians, or at least certain of their tribes (for there are great differences among them), if instead of coming in contact with the worst aspects of civilization, they had met with its better, gentler, and protective rather than destructive side, perhaps in the end they would have adapted themselves to it and would have been spared extinction. Civilization ought to be an extremely gentle teacher, however, and ought to bend a people gradually rather than break them suddenly. Permanent settlement and cultivation of the soil, which appear to be a necessity in the face of today's conditions, are a change in the Indian mode of life which is being forced upon tribes who are unprepared for it, instead of coming slowly as a natural consequence of gradual evolution.

It even seems to me that the scientific law concerning the inevitable extinction of peoples who resist civilization may be explained, not by the absolute incapacity of such peoples, but by the fact they do not have the time to civilize themselves as did the European peoples, that is, by means of continuous and gradual development. Living in a state of complete primitiveness, sometimes even in cannibalism, savage tribes suddenly are confronted with a highly developed and advanced civilization—in short, with a civilization which is absolutely too complex for their comprehension. Therefore, it is not at all surprising that, instead of being elevated and enlightened under its influence, they become bewildered and frantic, and end by dashing their heads against this civilization which is too tough for them to digest.

I return once again to the Indians. I have heard from experienced people and have become personally convinced that the Indian tribes possess a relatively high intellectual development. They are by no means inferior, for example, to the Kalmuks, Bashkirs, and other tribes who roam the steppes of Russia and Asia. They have their own traditions, their own mythology, and even their own poetry consisting of war songs, funeral songs, and the like. Some of their legends are even very cleverly composed and give evidence of a certain ingeniousness in making use of external observations of man and nature. According to one legend, when the Great Manitou decided to create man, he took clay, molded it in human form, and decided to bake it in the fire. But the first time he burned it to a coal-black color.

Nevertheless, he allowed his creation to live and thus originated the Negro. His second attempt was baked inadequately and the result was a white man. Only after the third attempt, taught by experience, was he able to strike the happy medium. He neither underbaked nor overbaked, and the result was a perfect creation, a truly beautiful red man.

In this legend there is a certain logic based upon an adroit utilization of the three colors of the human race. Furthermore, the speech of the Indians, full of comparisons and metaphors in the most ordinary conversation, is highly poetic and gives proof of a certain degree of mental maturity. In some individuals native intelligence is truly astounding and, generally speaking, all of them are very astute and are able to distinguish between truth and falsehood, even though sweetened to the highest degree. On the other hand, it is true that these traits are mingled with a naïveté that is practically childlike.

In conclusion, whatever may be said of these tribes, they have created a certain civilization of their own. They might progress even further and, with intelligent assistance, reach our own level of development—were it not for the fact that *our* civilization has discovered a much shorter road to progress: instead of encouraging and strengthening the weak, it exterminates them.

VII. A NATION OF IMMIGRANTS

Throughout the nineteenth century, immigrants from Europe flooded into the United States, some to work in factories, others to go west to find land for farming, all hoping to improve their lot in life as they had known it in Europe. Foreign visitors to America were keenly conscious of the immigrant element. As what sort of people did they see immigrants? What stereotypes did they perpetuate? What difficulties did the immigrant face in crossing the Atlantic? Did he receive any help adjusting to a new society? Establishing his identity as a *bona fide* American? When did the "American dream" bust for most immigrants? What positive contributions did immigrants make to American life? What negative contributions? What advice did the travelers give to people in Europe who were considering emigration?

Some of the earliest immigrants were of English, Irish, and German stock. They were observed by Captain Frederick Marryat, an English Tory who visited America in 1837-38. The following excerpt is taken from Marryat's Diary in America, with Remarks on its Institutions, *originally published in 1839, introduced by Sydney Jackson (New York: Alfred A. Knopf, 1962), pp. 393-95.*

It ought to be pointed out that among the emigrants are to be found the portion of the people in the United States the most disaffected and the most violent against England and its monarchical institutions, and who assist very much to keep up the feelings of dislike and ill-will which exist towards us. Nor is this to be wondered at; the happy and the wealthy do not go into exile; they are mostly disappointed and unhappy men, who attribute their misfortunes, often occasioned by their own imprudence, to any cause but the true one, and hate their own country and its institutions because they have been unfortunate in it. They form Utopian ideas of liberty and prosperity to be obtained by emigration; they discover that they have been deceived, and would willingly, if possible, return to the country they have abjured and the friends they have left behind. This produces an increase of irritation and ill-will, and they become the more violently vituperative in proportion as they feel the change.

I have had many conversations with English emigrants in the United States, and I never yet found one at all respectable who did not confess to me that he repented of emigration. One great cause of this is honourable to them: they feel that in common plain-dealing they are no match for the keen-witted, and I must add unprincipled, portion of the population with which they are thrown in contact. They must either sacrifice their principle or not succeed.

Many have used the same expression to me. "It is no use, sir, you must either turn regular Yankee and do as they do, or you have no chance of getting on in this country."

These people are much to be pitied; I used to listen to them with feelings of deep compassion. Having torn themselves away from old associations, and broken the links which should have bound them to their native soil, with the expectation of finding liberty, equality, and competence in a new country, they have discovered when too late that they have not a fraction of the liberty which is enjoyed in the country which they have left; that they have severed themselves from their friends to live amongst those with whom they do not like to associate; that they must now labour with their own hands, instead of employing others; and that the competence they expected, if it is to be obtained, must be so by a sacrifice of those principles of honesty and fair-dealing imbibed in their youth, adhered to in their manhood, but which, now that they have transplanted themselves, are gradually, although unwillingly, yielded up to the circumstances of their position.

I was once conversing with an Irishman; he was not very well pleased with his change; I laughed at him and said: "But here you are free, Paddy."—"Free!" replied he, "and pray who the devil was to buy or sell me when I was in Ireland? Free! och! that's talk; you're free to work as hard as a horse, and get but little for so doing."

The German emigrants are by far the most contented and well-behaved. They trouble themselves less about politics, associate with one another as much as possible, and when they take a farm, always, if they possibly can, get it in the neighbourhood of their own countrymen.

The emigrants most troublesome but, at the same time, the most valuable to the United States are the Irish. Without this class of people the Americans would not have been able to complete the canals and railroads and many other important works. They are, in fact, the principal labourers of the country, for the poor Germans who come out prefer being employed in any other way than in agriculture, until they amass sufficient to obtain farms of their own. As for the Irish, there are not many of them who possess land in the United States; the major portion of them remain labourers and die very little better off than when they went out. Some of them set up groceries (these are the most calculating and intelligent) and by allowing their countrymen to run in debt for liquor, etc., they obtain control over them, and make contracts with the government agents or other speculators (very advantageous to themselves) to supply so many men for public works; by these means a few acquire a great deal of money, while the many remain in comparative indigence.

We have been accustomed to ascribe the turbulence of the Irish lower classes to ill-treatment and a sense of their wrongs, but this disposition appears to follow them everywhere. It would be supposed that, having emigrated to America and obtained the rights of citizens, they would have amalgamated and fraternized to a certain degree with the people; but such is not the case; they hold themselves completely apart and distinct, living with their families in the same quarter of the city and adhering to their own manners and customs.

Another visitor from England, Miss Isabella Lucy Bird, also observed Irish and German immigrants in the middle years of the nineteenth century. In 1856, Miss Bird published The Englishwoman in America, *an account of her American travels two years earlier.*

The following excerpts are taken from the first London edition pp. 379-84.

Having seen the emigrants bid adieu to the Old World in the flurry of grief, hope, and excitement, I was curious to see what difference a five-weeks' voyage would have produced in them, and in what condition they would land upon the shores of America. In a city where emigrants land at the rate of a thousand a-day, I was not long of finding an opportunity. I witnessed the debarkation upon the shore of the New World of between 600 and 700 English emigrants, who had just arrived from Liverpool. If they looked tearful, flurried, and anxious when they left Liverpool, they looked tearful, pallid, dirty, and squalid when they reached New York. The necessary discomforts which such a number of persons must experience when huddled together in a close, damp, and ill-ventilated steerage, with very little change of clothing, and an allowance of water insufficient for the purposes of cleanliness, had been increased in this instance by the presence of cholera on board of the ship.

The wharfs at New York are necessarily dirty, and are a scene of indescribable bustle from morning to night, with ships arriving and sailing, ships loading and unloading, and emigrants pouring into the town in an almost incessant stream. They look as if no existing power could bring order out of such a chaos. In this crowd, on the shores of a strange land, the emigrants found themselves. Many were deplorably emaciated, others looked vacant and stupified. Some were ill, and some were penniless; but poverty and sickness are among the best recommendations which an emigrant can bring with him, for they place him under the immediate notice of those estimable and overworked men, the Emigration Commissioners, whose humanity is above all praise. These find him an asylum in the Emigrants' Hospital, on Ward's Island, and despatch him from thence in health, with advice and assistance for his future career. If he be in health, and have a few dollars in his pocket, he becomes the instantaneous prey of emigrant runners, sharpers, and keepers of groggeries; but of this more will be said hereafter.

A great many of these immigrants were evidently from country districts, and some from Ireland; there were a few Germans among them, and these appeared the least affected by the discomforts of the voyage, and by the novel and rather bewildering position in which they found themselves. They probably would feel more at home on first landing at New York than any of the others, for the lower part of the city is to a great extent inhabited by Germans, and at that time there were about 2000 houses where their favourite beverage, *lager-beer,* could be procured.

The goods and chattels of the Irish appeared to consist principally of numerous red-haired, unruly children, and ragged-looking bundles tied round with rope. The Germans were generally ruddy and stout, and took as much care of their substantial-looking, well-corded, heavy chests as though they contained gold. The English appeared pale and debilitated, and sat helpless and weary-looking on their large blue boxes. Here they found themselves in the chaotic confusion of this million-peopled city, not knowing whither to betake themselves, and bewildered by cries of "Cheap hacks!" "All aboard!" "Come to the cheapest house in all the world!" and invitations of a similar description. There were lodging-touters of every grade of dishonesty, and men with large placards were hurrying among the crowd, offering "palace" steamboats and "lightning express" trains, to whirl them at nominal rates to the Elysian Fields of the Far West. It is stated that six-tenths of these emigrants are attacked by fever soon after their arrival in the New World, but the provision for the sick is commensurate with the wealth and benevolence of New York.

Before leaving the city I was desirous to see some of the dwellings of the poor; I was therefore taken to what was termed a poor quarter. One house which I visited was approached from an entry, and contained ten rooms, which were let to different individuals and families. On the lowest floor was an old Irish widow, who had a cataract in one eye, and, being without any means of supporting herself, subsisted upon a small allowance made to her by her son, who was a carter. She was clean, but poorly dressed, and the room was scantily furnished. Except those who are rendered poor by their idleness and vices, it might have been difficult to find a poorer person in the city, I was told. Much sympathy was expressed for her, and for those who, like her, lived in this poor quarter. Yet the room was tolerably large, lofty, and airy, and had a window of the ordinary size of those in English dwelling-houses. For this room she paid four dollars or 16s.

per month, a very high rent. It was such a room as in London many a respectable clerk, with an income of 150*l.* a year, would think himself fortunate in possessing. . . .

It is a fact that no Golden Age exists on the other side of the water; that vice and crime have their penalties in America as well as in Europe; and that some of the worst features of the Old World are reproduced in the New. With all the desire that we may possess to take a sanguine view of things, there is something peculiarly hopeless about the condition of this class at New York, which in such a favourable state of society, and at such an early period of American history, has sunk so very low. The existence of a "dangerous class" at New York is now no longer denied. One person in seven of the whole population came under the notice of the authorities, either in the ranks of criminals or paupers, in 1852; and it is stated that last year the numbers reached an alarming magnitude, threatening danger to the peace of society. This is scarcely surprising when we take into consideration the numbers of persons who land in this city who have been expatriated for their vices, who are flying from the vengeance of outraged law, or who expect in the New World to be able to do evil without fear of punishment.

There are the idle and the visionary, who expect to eat without working; penniless demagogues, unprincipled adventurers, and the renegade outpourings of all Christendom; together with those who are enervated and demoralised by sickness and evil associates on board ship. I could not help thinking, as I saw many of the newly-arrived emigrants saunter helplessly into the groggeries, that, after spending their money, they would remain at New York, and help to swell the numbers of this class. These people live by their wits, and lose the little they have in drink. This life is worth very little to them; and in spite of Bible and Tract societies, and church missions, they know very little of the life to come; consequently they are ready for any mischief, and will imperil their existence for a small bribe.

A different set of immigrants were the Poles, who were described by one of their fellow countrymen, the novelist Henry Sienkiewicz. The author of Quo Vadis?, *Sienkiewicz visited America in 1876-78. The following passages are taken from* Portrait of America: Letters of Henry Sienkiewicz, *edited and translated by Charles Morley (New York, 1959), pp. 267-68, 270-74.*

My task is to give the readers a report on my visit to America, but the diverse manifestations of human life in this land make this no easy assignment. Indeed, should I be asked what kind of nation inhabits this country whose northern frontiers slumber under eternal snows and whose southern regions rustle with palm forests, my answer would be: there you will find not one nation but many nations—in fact, all the races of mankind. The Aryan, the Semite, the prognathic Negro, the son of the Celestial Empire with his slant eyes and long pigtail, and finally the original owner of these lands, the proud, red-skinned warrior—all of them live in the same climate, under the same skies, frequently side by side. There the Caucasian race has sent representatives of all of its branches and nationalities, beginning with the Greeks and ending with the Scots and the Irish.

To answer the question of how these national groups live together and what institutions were responsible for uniting them into a single political entity, I should have to follow in the footsteps of Alexis de Tocqueville and write an exhaustive treatise on American social institutions. For this I lack both talent and time. Therefore, I shall reply only with this generalization: in the United States there has been no attempt to assimilate or to force allegiance upon anyone, and therein lies the secret of the harmony in which the various elements live. This enigma can be explained by the single word "freedom"—a word which in Europe represents only an idea and a claim, but in the United States a practical reality.

It is the social, political, and religious freedom, the complete decentralization that stems from it, the loose political ties and unlimited respect for the individual which create the above-mentioned diversities and prevent the formation of a uniform national character. The relationship of the state to its citizens, the federal Constitution, the laws of the individual states, counties, and cities, the variety of social organizations, and a host of other matters—all of these are subjects too rich and too abundant for superficial treatment. Since it is impossible to follow several roads simultaneously without getting lost, I have selected the one that seemed to me the most interesting: the Poles and the Polish settlements in the United States.

On the ships sailing between Hamburg and New York there is a place even for the poorest passengers known as the steerage. On the English and French ships these accommodations are passable, but on the German vessels they are much inferior. Usually the steerage consists of a large dark room where the light of day enters not through windows opening along the deck, but through ordinary portholes in the ship's side. There are no cabins; the beds are attached directly to the wall; only a corner is assigned to the women and set off by a railing. When the sea is rough, the waves strike noisily against the portholes and fill the room with an ominous green light. Here the odors of the kitchen and the exhalations of human beings are mingled with the strong smell of ocean spray, tar, and wet rope. The air is heavy and damp and the room is dark. In the evenings lamps cast a dim light; glasses and tin utensils upon the tables tinkle from the rocking of the boat; the beams squeak; and from above are heard the angry shouting of the sailors and the shrill sounds of the petty officers' whistles. In such rooms as this the emigrants travel. . . .

Meanwhile, the days and nights pass. The ship with its prow pointed westward laboriously climbs wave after wave. It moves forward until at last, after a score of days or more, the land for which they had been heading begins to appear on the horizon as though emerging from the sea. The shores can now be seen ever more clearly. The quarantine house on Sandy Hook looms above the waves; further on, the enormous estuary of the East River can be perceived; still further, forests of masts, and beyond them a conglomeration of roofs, factory chimneys, and steeples. Over all of this rise columns of smoke unraveling in downy wisps at their summits. This is New York and its environs.

Our voyagers throng on deck, excited and happy. Whoever has crossed the ocean will easily comprehend their joy at the sight of land. Thus it seems to them that God has taken mercy upon them as upon some caravan lost in the desert, and having led them safely across the ocean, has shown them the promised land. Having grown accustomed to the silence and monotonous emptiness of the sea, they are now surrounded by the hum and noise of seething life. The small boat of the pilot rushes over the waves towards the ship with the swiftness of a swallow and it is followed by another from the quarantine office. The propeller begins to churn the water, pushing the ship first backward, then forward. You can hear the clanging of the unwinding winches, the shouting, calling, and cursing of the sailors. Another hour goes by. The ship eases its way into the narrow dock and disgorges its passengers. They have arrived! Through the large customs house located on the wharves they walk out into the street. And now what?

Matthew looks at Bartholomew, Bartholomew at Francis. What to do next? To whom should they turn? Where should they go? The ship had literally thrown them out on the street and that was the end. The agent in Hamburg had, of course, promised them that when they arrived there would be someone waiting for them, but that "someone" existed only in the words of the agent. The agent and the shipping company have fulfilled their obligations and owe the immigrants nothing more. The former had packed them into the steerage and the latter had transported them across the ocean. They may now do whatever they please. They have arrived in a metropolis. An unfamiliar life teems about them, elevated trains whistle above their heads, buses and carriages crisscross one another, crowds of white and colored persons hurry about with feverish speed in all directions, hucksters of every variety bellow as though possessed by the devil. And they—those peasants of ours—in the midst of this hubbub, splendor, and magnificence, feel even more lonely and foresaken than on the ocean wastes. Again they are at God's mercy. They have no conception of how much more they must endure before they encounter some Polish priest who will tell them which way to turn, where to secure employment, where to find a crust of bread. Even before this, greedy proprietors of boarding houses located close to the port will have squeezed the last penny out of them. They will have suffered cold in the filthy basements of various lodgings. Many a drunken Irishman, surprised at the size and strength of the Mazurian fist and anxious to test its power, will have blackened the eyes of these poor souls who dare not even defend themselves for fear of striking a "gentleman."

Their lot is a severe and terrifying one and whoever would depict it accurately would create an epic of human misery. To write or to hear of the days without a morsel of bread when hunger tears one's insides with an iron hand, of the nights spent on the docks under

the open heavens, and of the dreams interrupted by the humming of
mosquitoes in summer or the howling of the wind in winter, is easier
than to feel or to experience these things yourself. Is there anyone
whose hand is not against them? Their early history is a tale of misery,
loneliness, painful despair, and humiliation. Do not think, however,
that I am narrating the history of some particular group of Polish
immigrants. Not at all! Almost a hundred thousand peasants sent by
our land across the ocean have gone through such a Dantean infer-
no—in search of a better life. The Polish immigrants in America have
nothing in common with those living in France or Switzerland. The
latter are political exiles, expelled by revolutionary storms. In America
there are practically no Polish political *émigrés*. They are primarily
peasants and workers who have come in quest of bread. Thus you
will easily understand that in a country inhabited by a people who
are not at all sentimental, but rather energetic, industrious, and whose
competition it is difficult to survive, the fate of these newcomers,
poorly educated, unfamiliar with American conditions, ignorant of the
language, uncertain how to proceed, must truly be lamentable.

America or, strictly speaking, the United States, is not a land lack-
ing in hospitality. These coarse Yankee democrats, eternally occupied
with business, are at heart more generous than is superficially apparent. A healthy young man will almost invariably hear one piece of
advice: "Help yourself!" And if he does not know how to follow
this advice, he may even die of starvation. On the other hand, a man
who is old and infirm, a woman, or a child, receive more assistance
in the United States than anywhere else. This, however, is private
assistance which would be wholly inadequate in the case of immigrants. Yet if the government is to provide assistance, it must be in
the interest of the government to do so. Thus, for example, while
the influx of Chinese is dangerous to the young republic, that of white
immigrants is beneficial. The latter become citizens, they settle on
the land and transform the prairie into arable fields, they found towns,
establish new trade relations, and contribute to economic expansion.
It is, therefore, in the interest of the Union to encourage European
immigration.

That is the purpose of the immigrant homes in New York where
the new arrivals can find shelter, food, and instruction in the English

language and in some handicraft. The work done by the immigrants in these houses covers the cost of their maintenance. After a certain period when the immigrant is prepared for the struggle with life, he leaves the establishment and begins to work on his own.

But such institutions, giving creditable evidence of the wisdom and generosity of the Americans, are entirely inadequate. To begin with, these institutions cannot accommodate even half the immigrants who need shelter. Secondly, only trades are taught in them while many immigrants, especially the Poles, yearn for the soil. Furthermore, these establishments are a form of guardianship, in fact, regular work-houses. Men, women, and children work there separately, according to the nature of their skills; thus, families cannot remain together. For these reasons and because of the aversion of our peasants to all similar institutions such as hospitals, workhouses, and the like, very few of them take advantage of the immigrant houses.

But the main reason is that our peasants know nothing of the existence of these institutions. I happened to meet some Poles who had already been living in the United States for several years and who learned of the existence of immigrant workhouses only when, in conversation, the expression fell from my lips. Then, too, the immigrant houses do not have their own agents, as do the hotels, to hunt out the new arrivals in the port.

And yet, is there nothing that our peasants bring to the New World that might guarantee them a peaceful life and a secure livelihood? Of course there is! They bring with them the habit of being content with little, true peasant endurance, patience, and an iron constitution. A German or French immigrant overcomes only with difficulty those hardships and inconveniences to which our peasant adjusts himself with ease, accustomed as he is to walking barefoot, eating whatever is at hand, and sleeping under any kind of roof. He does not even comprehend the need for various comforts that the German and French immigrant regard as necessities of life. Sun does not burn him; rain does not harm him; snow and wind do not chill him. In cold Wisconsin and Minnesota he is not perturbed by the snow drifts; in semitropical Texas, once he throws off the fever, he works in the scorching heat like a Negro. Perhaps he may be less skillful than others, but he has greater endurance and is a humble and quiet worker.

Many American cities became known as "immigrant cities" because of the overwhelming number of foreigners who came to work in factories. Lawrence, Massachusetts, for example, was filled with Irish, English, and French Canadian labor. An English manufacturer, James Burnley, from Bradford, Yorkshire, visited Lawrence in 1879 and recorded his impressions in Two Sides of the Atlantic *(London, 1880), pp. 62-63, 64-67.*

Lawrence is sometimes called the Bradford of America, for it is there that Bradford Americans come out the strongest. It is the chief seat of the worsted manufacture in America, and, naturally, it is the place to which the Bradford emigrant-weavers mostly flock. Bradford faces meet you in the streets, Bradford saloon keepers supply you with your glass of lager, Bradford people stand behind the counters of the shops, Bradford names stare out from numerous sign-boards in the principal street, and, once get inside a factory, it is Bradford, Bradford everywhere. If it had not been for Bradford, indeed, Lawrence would hardly have made the success it has, for not only has Bradford supplied a large proportion of the operatives, but it has supplied much of the technical skill and managerial capacity which have enabled Lawrence to attain its present high standing in the manufacturing world. What could Lawrence have done, too, without Bradford machinery? As you walk through the long rooms of the mills, the familiar names of Bradford and Keighley makers can be read on the combing, carding, and other machines; indeed, Bradford's sign manual is written so palpably upon everything in and around these factories, that you can almost imagine that you are still at home. . . .

Coming, however, to the factory workers generally—the hands who do the real labour—we find them little, if any, better off than the same class of workpeople in England. Formerly, when wages were high and workers more scarce, it was different. In the preparing (carding and drawing) rooms, the women earn from 80 cents to a dollar per day; weavers earn from a dollar to one dollar and thirty cents; boys and girls from 50 to 80 cents; and children at from eight to twelve or thirteen years of age, 25 to 40 or 50 cents a day. These wages are something like the average. There are establishments paying better wages—but not many—and there are establishments where the rate of remuneration is lower. Now, when we come to set against this the fact that the cost of living is really much higher in America than in England, we get to this undoubted truth, that the factory workers of the United States are not any better off than those of our own country. I shall have more to say in my next chapter on this head, however, and upon the boarding-house system which prevails to such a large extent in connection with the American factories; but I may at present observe that at the boarding-houses, where living may be presumed to be the cheapest, men pay four dollars and women two dollars and seventy-five cents per week. All kinds of clothing are much dearer than on this side of the Atlantic. Now, when we come to strike a balance between the income and the outgo of these factory workers, we find that the surplus in hand is little, if any, over that which the Bradford factory workers find themselves in possession of at the end of each week. When the worker is also a housekeeper and has a family dependent upon him, his condition is still worse, as, first and foremost, there is the item of house-rent to be taken into consideration, which may be safely set down as double that which he would have to pay in England for very much superior accommodation. In America, rent is reckoned as about one-fourth of a family's household expenses; in England it may be set down as perhaps an eighth. The English factory worker who goes over to America with the intention of continuing to toil in the mill will find therefore that he does not materially improve his position—*i.e.,* as things are at present. He will have to work harder, to put up with fewer home-comforts, and will to some extent experience the loneliness and the disadvantage of being a foreigner. On the other hand, he will breathe a purer atmosphere, he will have a greater variety of eatables, and, perhaps, he will feel somewhat more independent.

The Americans do not take well to factory labour, as a rule. At the Pacific Mills about one-third of the workpeople are American, the rest are foreign. "You see," said a certain manager to me, "the American is too well educated to take to hard work like this. He can put his brains to better use." Be that as it may, the fact remains, that the majority of factory hands in America are imported from England. While trade has been so bad in the States, much ill-feeling has been engendered between the various nationalities engaged in factory and other labour, the classes which were satisfied to accept the lowest pay being strongly despised by those who demanded a higher price. The Canadian Frenchman, who is vulgarly styled a "Cannook," is the workman who is at the bottom of the scale. He can afford to work for the smallest wage because he can live cheaper than any one else. Indeed, he can live well and be happy on what would hardly keep an Englishman from starvation and utter wretchedness. He can defy natural and sanitary laws with an impunity which entitles him to be classed with the beasts of the field. I was told of instances where as many as fourteen or fifteen of these people lived together in one wooden tenement of three rooms. The German is almost the equal of the "Cannook" in point of frugality, but he is not so piggish in his home and habits; besides, the Fatherlander makes himself sociable—drinks his lager, and enjoys himself at his Verein like a man. The German and the Englishman get on together in America better than any other two nationalities. The Irishman is quite as swinish as the "Cannook," but he cannot live so cheaply, being of a more excitable and lively turn. He must have his whisky; while the "Cannook" is quite content to drink the lowest-priced gin. The Canadian Frenchman really is about as big a bugbear in the New England cities and towns as the Heathen Chinee is in California, and, "which I may beg to remark," his smile is less "childlike and bland." Nor is the negro held in much better repute as a workman in these districts. Two coloured men were tramping through Holyoke the day I was there, and the good people of that city—at least, a few of them—stoned the poor fellows away. They were determined not to let the niggers settle down there, at all events. There is yet a great labour battle to be fought in America, and with all these nationalities and complicated feelings and interests to contend against there is much reason for apprehension.

Europeans who took the transcontinental railroad to the West Coast in the second half of the nineteenth century usually commented on the Chinese immigrants in San Francisco. A Scottish feminist, Miss Emily Faithfull, visited America in 1872, 1882, and 1884. In her Three Visits to America *(New York, 1884), pp. 220-23, she described "China Town."*

I arrived in San Francisco just in time to visit the Chinese quarter during the New Year festivities of the "Celestials." Strange indeed to English eyes were the mottoes and devices painted on the sign-boards of the various stores—"Hop Wo," "Tin Yuk," "Hang Hi," "Chung Sun," "Shan Tong." The Chinese doctors hang out boards, on one of which we found "Yeang Tsz Zing feels the pulse and heals the most difficult and unheard-of diseases." Wholesale dealers in opium hang out red cards with appropriate scrolls; the "Fan Tan" saloons have their insignias, such as "Get rich and please come in," tempting the passer to try his luck at the game of chance. We visited several of the stores belonging to the leading merchants, and found them clad in long robes and silken trousers. They receive visitors with the salutation, "Kong hi fat choy," an equivalent to our "Happy New Year." Then we went to the Josh Houses or temples, which contained some fine specimens of carving, embroidery, and bronzes, and such extraordinary idols, before whom are spread roasted pig and chicken, with sweetmeats and cups of tea, while lamps burn in the midst. The air is full of the smell of the incense from sandal-wood, mingled with the fumes of opium pipes. Worship takes place at no set time; the Chinaman performs his devotions at his own bidding, except on the birthday of the gods. So you see in the temples the strange spectacle of one man apparently muttering prayers before some ugly-looking idol, another is consulting the Josh by balancing bamboo splints, and a third is prostrating himself on the ground before a tinsel image. Kwan Tai seems the favorite deity, and is adorned with a long black beard and a very red face. Wah Tah is the god of medicine, and holds a coated pill in his hand, while Tsoi Pak Shing Kwun is the god of wealth, and appropriately wields a bar of bullion. On the first and fifteenth of the month the married women pay special devotion to the goddess of mercy, whom they hold in great veneration. There is happily much missionary work now going on in this city; churches and schools have been opened specially for the Chinese, and I was invited to a home where Chinese women are taught sewing and useful occupations by ladies who endeavor at the same time to redeem them from paganism.

In the evening during these New Year carousals, China-town presented a very gay appearance, being illuminated with Chinese lanterns. We were nearly suffocated with the fire-crackers which were exploded

on all sides in such a wholesale manner that I expected the city itself
would be on fire. But the strangest sight of all is the Chinese theatre.
The plays take about three weeks in representation; the discordant
orchestra is ensconced in an alcove at the back of the stage; there
is "no curtain," no scenery, no female performers, and if an actor
is slain he lies on the floor for a minute, and then gets up and walks
away. The acrobatic feats, which are introduced on every possible
occasion, are simply marvellous. No wonder that one of the Girards
gained his inspiration from this source. The costumes are gorgeous
and grotesque in the extreme, and a very short stay at this peculiar
entertainment is quite sufficient for the most stage-struck English
playgoer. The Chinaman, like the Mormon, indulges in polygamy,
and the "small feet" wives are never seen on the streets. Champagne
and choice confections are pressed on the visitors at this season, and
the festivities are kept up for several days, during which time business
is quite suspended.

For the most part it must be confessed that Chinatown is a filthy
place, and yet, singular to relate, the Chinese, as a rule, are very
clean in their own persons. I have seen the bedroom of a Chinese
cook in a friend's house, which was not only scrupulously well kept,
but daintily decorated with flowers. The bed was white as snow, and
though the room was only the size of an ordinary steamer cabin, it
was screened off by a colored curtain, his absolutely clean change
of raiment hung on a peg; beside this, on the table was a vase of
lilies, and not a speck of dust could be detected anywhere. The "hood-
lums"—the name for the California *gamin*—chase and ridicule these
poor half-shaved, almond-eyed "celestials," with their inexpressive
faces, queer pigtails, brown skin, jet-black hair, clad in loose garments
and wooden shoes, and with pantaloons made tight to the ankle with
white bandages. If they were new importations into the country these
wretched boys could not hoot at them more vehemently when they
meet them off their own special ground. There the hoodlum would
undoubtedly get the worst of it, and with commendable wisdom the
little cowards wait their opportunity elsewhere.

It is no wonder that a city of such vast distances as San Francisco
claims the honor of having introduced the use of cable cars, which
run in such a truly mysterious fashion that the newly-imported
Chinaman's remark, "No pushee, no pullee, go like hellee," best

describes their rapid transit through the streets, and up the steep hills, for which this town is famous.

Upon returning to the Old Country after their travels in the United States, Europeans often lectured or wrote pamphlets and books advising their countrymen on who should emigrate, where they should go in America, and what they could expect to find. Following a brief jaunt in 1883, an Englishman, Thomas Greenwood, gave advice to would-be emigrants in A Tour in the States & Canada. Out and Home in Six Weeks *(London, 1883), pp. 157-160.*

America is not by any means an Eldorado for all. There could be found in New York as much poverty as there is in London, and the overcrowding of dwelling-houses in the districts inhabited by the working classes would provide in many cases quite as appalling facts as could be found in St. Giles's or Whitechapel. There are at the present time in the leading cities of the States quite as many unemployed as may be found in many English towns. There has been some exaggeration in the prospects held out to those who contemplate finding a new home, and there are some industries which are greatly overdone in America. It is just as possible to do well in England as America; and success there is dependent on just the same qualities as are necessary here. Of unskilled labour there is enough and to spare in America. The old saying must again be used, that a man with a trade in his hands stands a hundred per cent better chance there than one who has not. American industries are progressing at a rapid rate, and there is room in them for men of skill and industry, with good remuneration for their work, and a social position higher than would be their corresponding status here. Whatever a man's trade is in the States is no barrier to his social progress. Labour is honoured highly, as all the world over it ought to be, if honestly followed.

My own view is that, comparing the two countries, there is a better and quicker return for the same amount of capital or labour in the States than is possible in the majority of cases here.

The feeling that there is scope in the States obtains possession of the mind of the man who goes out determined to make his way. Willingness to work and to take the work which presents itself ought to be dominant. Several cases come to my mind that I know personally. A friend of mine had an excellent training as a mechanical engineer, crossed the Atlantic, and is doing favourably as a store keeper and small farmer, killing his pigs himself and taking all such work as part of the day's labour. Another was unsuccessful in business on his own account, in one of the midland towns of England, and is now a manager of works in the trade in which he was engaged here, at an excellent salary, and bids fair to be a partner by-and-bye, without any large investment, his knowledge and skill in the business being accepted as the equivalent of capital. For those who have good situations in this country, to give them up for the sake of change, with the idea of doing better out there, is not by any means advisable. On the other hand, for unmarried young men, with plenty of energy, and who like work for its own sake, there is plenty of room; and such, with tact, push and principle, the great motto of Abraham Lincoln, would scarcely fail to get on.

Let me here give one practical suggestion to those who comtemplate going out and who have a trade in their hands. Advertise for what employment you are seeking in the journal representing your particular trade. Class papers are prolific in America, and are largely read, and used for the purpose of bringing employer and employé together.

America is full of schoolmasters, tutors, professors of music, languages, and other arts. For clever and original designers there is a demand. In the engineering and hardware trade there is a good scope. The chemical industries are rapidly developing, and those who have a good and trustworthy knowledge of the making of chemicals for manufacturing purposes would find room for their labours. I have already referred to the jewellery and silver trade. The shirt, collar, and clothing trades are overstocked, excepting, perhaps, as regards hats. Saddlery and harness makers find remunerative employment. Printers are in demand, but, before such could find good employment, they would require to get well accustomed to the American ideas of display. In the Birmingham and Sheffield trades there are openings for labour.

With whatever capital a person emigrates, and none should go without some, he should prefer to err in being over cautious rather than prematurely confident. There are all manner of methods for ridding a new comer of his stock of wealth if he be not wide awake. A short time spent in reconnoitring after arrival would be advisable to most, but in few cases is it well to attempt settling down in New York. Other cities present far better opportunities than that one, which unfortunately receives a good deal of scum from every part of the world.

I know nothing of the value of land and the practical prospects of farming, but I do know that farming there is very different from what it is here. It may be rough and primitive there when compared with scientific farming here, but it is, at all events, more likely of success. Untold millions of acres yet remain to be cultivated, and here I will quote a few figures. Of the 220,000,000 acres of land in Ohio, Indiana, Illinois, Michigan, and Wisconsin, about 90,000,000 are under cultivation, and 70,000,000 consists of forests and sandy plains, the other 60,000,000 being still available for colonisation. There are in the States of Kansas, Nebraska, and Minnesota 160,000,000 acres, 12,000,000 of which are under cultivation, while 78,000,000 might be cultivated at a large profit and a very small preliminary outlay. Texas has 200,000,000 acres, but the greater part has hitherto been used chiefly for grazing, yet there are at least 60,000,000 acres which might with advantage be planted with corn and cotton. In the territories of Montana, Wyoming, and Dakota there are about 120,000,000 acres of very good land, nearly the whole of which is at present uncultivated and can be obtained on very easy terms.

In the purchasing of land every care and caution will require to be exercised. The literature of the various land companies must not always be accepted without question. They naturally speak graphically and enthusiastically about what they are desirous of selling.

In the towns living is very much dearer than in England. Money has not the same purchasing value there as here. Rents are notoriously high, and it may safely be said that an average rent in New York would swallow up of itself an average salary on this side.

The immense increase in the emigration returns for the last few years, from what can be gathered, has not perceptibly overstocked the market. Some writers in Germany have been making a great deal recently of the fact of some German emigrants returning to their native districts with disappointed hopes, but it is patent that official Germany does not relish this drain of the bone and sinew of the country, glad to find a home in the Far West where conscription cannot follow them.

The population of the United States at the last census was

50,155,783, and there is yet room for some five or six times the number, so far as the size of the country is concerned. For her vast absorbing power Europe owes a debt of gratitude to her, and she is fulfilling her duty to Europe very faithfully, and to British people especially she holds out a very welcome hand.

VIII. THE STRENGTHS AND WEAKNESSES OF AMERICAN DEMOCRACY

As de Tocqueville's *Democracy in America* towers above all other attempts to explain the political institutions and social relations in American life during the first half of the nineteenth century, James Bryce's *American Commonwealth* is similarly preëminent for the second half of the century. Bryce visited the United States in 1870, 1881, 1883-84, and 1887, familiarizing himself with every corner of the land. More importantly, he immersed himself in the study of American history and politics. In 1888 he published his classic three-volume treatise, *The American Commonwealth*, which was revised and republished several times before his death in 1922. In the following excerpts, from a two-volume edition (London, 1889), vol. 2, pp. 451-67, 469-73, is Bryce more critical of the system or the leaders of American democracy? How does he relate the two? What connection does he see between government and business interests? How does he explain the American respect for the law? How does his depiction of American patriotism compare with de Tocqueville's? Is Bryce generally optimistic or pessimistic concerning the future of America?

The word Democracy is often used to mean a spirit or tendency, sometimes the spirit of revolution, sometimes the spirit of equality. For our present purpose it is better to take it as denoting simply a form of government, that in which the numerical majority rules, deciding questions of state by the votes, whether directly, as in the ancient republics, or mediately, as in modern representative government, of the body of citizens, the citizens being if not the whole, at least a very large proportion of the adult males. We may properly begin by asking, What are the evils to which we may expect such a form of government to be exposed?

Firstly, a certain commonness of mind and tone, a want of dignity and elevation in and about the conduct of public affairs, an insensibility to the nobler aspects and finer responsibilities of national life.

Secondly, a certain apathy among the luxurious classes and fastidious minds, who find themselves of no more account than the ordinary voter, and are disgusted by the superficial vulgarities of public life.

Thirdly, a want of knowledge, tact, and judgment in the details of legislation, as well as in administration, with an inadequate recognition of the difficulty of these kinds of work, and of the worth of special experience and skill in dealing with them. Because it is imcompetent, the multitude will not feel its incompetence, and will not seek or defer to the counsels of those who possess the requisite capacity.

Fourthly, laxity in the management of public business. The persons entrusted with such business being only average men, thinking themselves and thought of by others as average men, with a deficient sense of their high responsibilities, may succumb to the temptations which the control of legislation and the public funds present, in cases where persons of a more enlarged view and with more of a social reputation to support would remain incorruptible. To repress such derelictions of duty is every citizen's duty, but for that reason it is in large communities apt to be neglected. Thus the very causes which implant the mischief favour its growth.

The above-mentioned tendencies are all more or less observable in the United States. As each of them has been described already in its proper place, a summary reference may here be sufficient to indicate their relation to the democratic form of government and to the immanent spirit or theory which lies behind that form.

The tone of public life is lower than one expects to find it in so great a nation. Just as we assume that an individual man will at any supreme moment in his own life rise to a higher level than that on which he usually moves, so we look to find those who conduct the affairs of a great state inspired by a sense of the magnitude of the interests entrusted to them. Their horizon ought to be expanded, their feeling of duty quickened, their dignity of attitude enhanced. Human nature with all its weaknesses does show itself capable of being thus roused on its imaginative side; and in Europe, where the traditions of aristocracy survive, everybody condemns as mean or unworthy acts done or language held by a great official which would pass unnoticed in a private citizen. It is the principle of *noblesse oblige* with the sense of duty and trust substituted for that of mere hereditary rank.

Such a sentiment is comparatively weak in America. A cabinet minister, or senator, or governor of a State, sometimes even a President, hardly feels himself more bound by it than the director of a railway company or the mayor of a town does in Europe. Not assuming himself to be individually wiser, stronger, or better than his fellow-citizens, he acts and speaks as though he were still simply one of them, and so far from magnifying his office and making it honourable, seems anxious to show that he is the mere creature of the popular vote, so filled by the sense that it is the people and not he who governs as to fear that he should be deemed to have forgotten his personal insignificance. There is in the United States abundance of patriotism, that is to say, of a passion for the greatness and happiness of the Republic, and a readiness to make sacrifices for it. The history of the Civil War showed that this passion is at least as strong as in England or France. There is no want of an appreciation of the collective majesty of the nation, for this is the theme of incessant speeches, nor even of the past and future glories of each particular State in the Union. But these sentiments do not bear their appropriate fruit in raising the conception of public office, of its worth and its dignity. The newspapers assume public men to be selfish and cynical. Disinterested virtue is not looked for, is perhaps turned into ridicule where it exists. The hard commercial spirit which pervades the meetings of a joint-stock company is the spirit in which most politicians speak of public business, and are not blamed for speaking. Something, especially in the case of newspapers, must be allowed for the humorous tendencies of the American mind, which likes to put forward the absurd and even vulgar side of things for the sake of getting fun out of them. But after making such allowances, the fact remains that, although no people is more emotional, and even in a sense more poetical, in no country is the ideal side of public life, what one may venture to call the heroic element in a public career, so ignored by the mass and repudiated by the leaders. This affects not only the elevation but the independence and courage of public men; and the country suffers from the want of what we call distinction in its conspicuous figures. . . .

A state must of course take the people as it finds them, with such elements of ignorance and passion as exists in masses of men everywhere. Nevertheless a representative or parliamentary system provides the means of mitigating the evils to be feared from ignorance or haste, for it vests the actual conduct of affairs in a body of specially chosen and presumably specially qualified men, who may themselves entrust such of their functions as need peculiar knowledge or skill to a smaller governing body or bodies selected in respect of their more eminent fitness. By this method the defects of democracy are remedied, while its strength is retained. The masses give their impulse to the representatives: the representatives, directed by the people to secure certain ends, bring their skill and experience to bear on the choice and application of the best means. The Americans, however, have not so constructed or composed their representative bodies as to secure a large measure of these benefits. The legislatures are disjoined from the administrative offices. The members of legislatures are not chosen for their ability or experience, but are, five-sixths of them, little above the average citizen. They are not much respected or trusted, and finding nothing exceptional expected from them, they behave as ordinary men. The separation of the executive from the legislature is a part of the constitutional arrangements of the country, and has no doubt some advantages. The character of the legislatures is due to a mistaken view of human equality and an exaggerated devotion to popular sovereignty. It is a result of democratic theory pushed to extremes, but is not necessarily incident to a democratic government. The government of England, for instance, has now become substantially a democracy, but there is no reason why it should imitate America in either of the points just mentioned, nor does democratic France, apt enough to make a bold use of theory, seem to have pushed theory to excess in these particular directions. I do not, however, deny that a democratic system makes the people self-confident, and that self-confidence may easily pass into a jealousy of delegated power, an undervaluing of skill and knowledge, a belief that any citizen is good enough for any political work. This is perhaps more likely to happen with a people who have really reached a high level of political competence: and so one may say that the reason why the American democracy is not better is because it is so good. Were it less educated, less shrewd, less actively interested in public affairs, less independent in spirit, it might be more disposed, like the masses in Europe, to look up to the classes which have hitherto done the work of governing. So perhaps the excellence of rural local self-government has lowered the conception of national government. The ordinary American farmer or shopkeeper or artisan bears a part in the local government of his township or village, or county, or small municipality. He is quite competent to discuss the questions that arise there. He knows his fellow-citizens, and can, if he takes the trouble, select the fittest of them for local office. No high standard of fitness is needed, for the work of local administration can be adequately despatched by any sensible man of business habits. Taking his ideas from this local government, he images Congress to himself as nothing more than a larger town council or board of county commissioners, the President and his Cabinet as a sort of bigger mayor and city treasurer and education superintendent; he is therefore content to choose for high Federal posts such persons as he would elect for these local offices. They are such as he is himself; and it would seem to him a disparagement of his own civic worth were he to deem his neighbours, honest, hard-working, keen-witted men, unfit for any places in the service of the Republic.

The comparative indifference to political life of the educated and wealthy classes which is so much preached at by American reformers and dwelt on by European critics is partly due to this attitude of the multitude. These classes find no smooth and easy path lying before them. Since the masses do not look to them for guidance, they do not come forward to give it. If they wish for office they must struggle for it, avoiding the least appearance of presuming on their social position. . . . .

The Spoils System reminds us of the Machine and the whole organization of Rings and Bosses. This is the ugliest feature in the current politics of the country. Must it be set down to democracy? To some extent, yes. It could not have grown up save in a popular government; and some of the arrangements which have aided its growth, such as the number and frequency of elections, have been dictated by what may be called the narrow doctrinarism of democracy. But these arrangements are not essential to the safety of the government; and the other causes which have brought about the machine politics of cities seem to be preventible causes. The city masses may improve if immigration declines, offices may cease to be the reward of party victory, the better citizens may throw themselves more actively into political work. . . .

Of the deficiencies summarized in this chapter, those which might seem to go deepest, because they have least to do with the particular constitutional arrangements of the country, and are most directly the offspring of its temper and habits, are the prominence of inferior men in politics and the absence of distinguished figures. The people are good, but not good enough to be able to dispense with efficient service by capable representatives and officials, wise guidance by strong and enlightened leaders. But they are neither well served or well led. If it were clear that these are the fruits of liberty and equality, the prospects of the world would be darker than we have been wont to think them. They are the fruits not of liberty and equality, but of an optimism which has underrated the inherent difficulties of politics and failings of human nature, of a theory which has confused equality of civil rights and duties with equality of capacity, and of a thoughtlessness which has forgotten that the problems of the world and the dangers which beset society are always putting on new faces appearing in new directions. The Americans started their Republic with a determination to prevent abuses of power such as they had suffered from the British Crown. Freedom seemed the one thing necessary; and freedom was thought to consist in cutting down the powers of legislatures and officials. Freedom was the national boast during the years that followed down till the Civil War, and in the delight of proclaiming themselves superior in this regard to the rest of the world they omitted to provide themselves with the other requisites for good government, and forgot that power may be abused in other ways than by monarchic tyranny or legislative usurpation. They continued to beat the drum along the old ramparts erected in 1776 and 1789 against George III., or those who might try to imitate him, when the enemy had moved quite away from that side of the position, and was beginning to threaten their rear. No maxim was more popular among them than that which declares external vigilance to be the price of freedom. Unfortunately their vigilance took account only of the old dangers, and did not note the development of new ones, as if the captain of a man-of-war were to think only of his guns and armour-plating, and neglect to protect himself against torpedoes. Thus abuses were suffered to grow up, which seemed trivial in the midst of so general a prosperity; and good citizens who were occupied in other and more engrossing ways, allowed politics to fall into the hands of mean men. The efforts which these citizens are now making to recover the control of public business would have encountered fewer obstacles had they been made sooner. But the obstacles will be overcome. No one, I think, who has studied either the history of the American people, or their present mind and habits, will conclude that there is among them any jealousy of merit, any positive aversion to culture or knowledge. Neither the political arrangements nor the social and economical conditions of the country tend at this moment to draw its best intellects and loftiest characters into public life. But the democratic temper of the people does not stand in the way.

The commonest of the old charges against democracy was that it passed into ochlocracy. I have sought to show that this has not happened, and is not likely to happen in America. The features of mob-rule do not appear in her system, whose most characteristic faults are the existence of a class of persons using government as a means of private gain and the menacing power of wealth. Plutocracy, which the ancients contrasted with democracy, has shown in America an inauspicious affinity for certain professedly democratic institutions.

Perhaps no form of government needs great leaders so much as democracy. The fatalistic habit of mind perceptible among the Americans needs to be corrected by the spectacle of courage and independence taking their own path, and not looking to see whither the mass are moving. Those whose material prosperity tends to lap them in self-complacency and dull the edge of aspiration, need to be thrilled by the emotions which great men can excite, stimulated by the ideals they present, stirred to a loftier sense of what national life may attain. In some countries men of brilliant gifts may be dangerous to freedom; but the ambition of American statesmen has been schooled to flow in constitutional channels, and the Republic is strong enough to stand any strain to which the rise of heroes may expose her.

Those merits of American government which belong to its Federal

Constitution have been already discussed: we have now to consider such as flow from the rule of public opinion, from the temper, habits, and ideas of the people.

I. The first is that of Stability.—As one test of a human body's soundness is its capacity for reaching a great age, so it is high praise for a political system that it has stood no more changed than any institution must change in a changing world, and that it now gives every promise of durability. The people are profoundly attached to the form which their national life has taken. The Federal Constitution is, to their eyes, an almost sacred thing, an Ark of the Covenant, whereon no man may lay rash hands. Everywhere in Europe one hears schemes of radical change freely discussed. There is a strong monarchical party in France, a republican party in Italy and Spain. There are anarchists in Germany and Russia. Even in England, it is impossible to feel confident that any one of the existing institutions of the country will be standing fifty years hence. But in the United States the discussion of political problems busies itself with details and assumes that the main lines must remain as they are for ever. This conservative spirit, jealously watchful even in small matters, sometimes prevents reforms, but it assures to the people an easy mind, and a trust in their future which they feel to be not only a present satisfaction but a reservoir of strength.

The best proof of the well-braced solidity of the system is that it survived the Civil War, changed only in a few points which have not greatly affected the balance of National and State powers. Another must have struck every European traveller who questions American publicists about the institutions of their country. When I first travelled in the United States, I used to ask thoughtful men, superior to the prejudices of custom, whether they did not think the States' system defective in such and such points, whether the legislative authority of Congress might not profitably be extended, whether the suffrage ought not to be restricted as regards negroes or immigrants, and so forth. Whether assenting or dissenting, the persons questioned invariably treated such matters as purely speculative, saying that the present arrangements were far too deeply rooted for their alteration to come within the horizon of practical politics. So when a serious trouble arises, a trouble which in Europe would threaten revolution, the people face it quietly, and assume that a tolerable solution will be found.

At the disputed election of 1876, when each of the two great parties, heated with conflict, claimed that its candidate had been chosen President, and the Constitution supplied no way out of the difficulty, public tranquillity was scarcely disturbed, and the public funds fell but little. A method was invented of settling the question which both sides acquiesced in, and although the decision was a boundless disappointment to the party which had cast the majority of the popular vote, that party quietly submitted to lose those spoils of office whereon its eyes had been feasting.

II. Feeling the law to be its own work, the people is disposed to obey the law.—In a preceding chapter I have examined occasional instances of the disregard of the law, and the supersession of its tardy methods by the action of the crowd. Such instances scarcely affect the credit which the Americans are specially eager to claim of being a law-abiding community. It is the best result that can be ascribed to the direct participation of the people in their government that they have the love of the maker for his work, that every citizen looks upon a statute as a regulation made by himself for his own guidance no less than for that of others, every official as a person he has himself chosen, and whom it is therefore his interest, with no disparagement to his personal independence, to obey. Plato thought that those who felt their own sovereignty would be impatient of all control: nor is it to be denied that the principle of equality may result in lowering the status and dignity of a magistrate. But as regards law and order the gain much exceeds the loss, for every one feels that there is no appeal from the law, behind which there stands the force of the nation. Such a temper can exist and bear these fruits only where minorities, however large, have learned to submit patiently to majorities, however small. But that is the one lesson which the American government through every grade and in every department daily teaches, and which it has woven into the texture of every citizen's mind. The habit of living under a rigid constitution superior to ordinary statutes—indeed two rigid constitutions, since the State Constitution is a fundamental law within its own sphere no less than is the Federal—intensifies this legality of view, since it may turn all sorts of questions which have not been determined by a direct vote of the people into questions of legal construction. It even accustoms people to submit to see their direct vote given in the enactment of a State Constitution nullified by the decision of a court holding that the Federal Constitution has been contravened. Every page of American history illustrates the wholesome results. The events of the last few years present an instance of the constraint which the people put on themselves in order to respect every form of law. The Mormons, a community not exceeding 140,000 persons, persistently defied all the efforts of Congress to root out polygamy, a practice eminently repulsive to American notions. If they inhabited a State, Congress could not have interfered at all, but as Utah is only a Territory, Congress has a power of legislating for it which overrides Territorial ordinances passed by the local legislature. Thus they were really at the mercy of Congress, had it chosen to employ violent methods. But by entrenching themselves behind the letter of the Constitution, they continued for many years to maintain their "peculiar institution" by evading the statutes passed against it and challenging a proof which under the common law rules of evidence it has been usually found impossible to give. Vehement declaimers hounded on Congress to take arbitrary means for the suppression of the practice, but Congress and the executive submitted to be outwitted rather than exceed their proper province, and succeeded at last (if indeed they have completely succeeded) only by a statute whose searching but moderate and strictly constitutional provisions the recalcitrants failed to evade. The same spirit of legality shows itself in misgoverned cities. Even where it is notorious that officials have been chosen by the grossest fraud and that they are robbing the city, the body of the people, however indignant, recognize the authority, and go on paying the taxes which a Ring levies, because strict legal proof of the frauds and robberies is not forthcoming. Wrong-doing supplies a field for the display of virtue.

III. There is a broad simplicity about the political ideas of the people, and a courageous consistency in carrying them out in practice. When they have accepted a principle, they do not shrink from applying it "right through," however disagreeable in particular cases some of the results may be. I am far from meaning that they are logical in the French sense of the word. They have little taste either for assuming abstract propositions or for syllogistically deducing practical conclusions therefrom. But when they have adopted a general maxim of policy or rule of action they show more faith in it than the English for instance would do, they adhere to it where the English would make exceptions, they prefer certainty and uniformity to the advantages which might occasionally be gained by deviation. If this tendency is partly the result of obedience to a rigid constitution, it is no less due to the democratic dislike of exceptions and complexities, which the multitude finds not only difficult of comprehension but disquieting to the individual who may not know how they will affect him. Take for instance the boundless freedom of the press. There are abuses obviously incident to such freedom, and these abuses have not failed to appear. But the Americans deliberately hold that in view of the benefits which such freedom on the whole promises, abuses must be borne with and left to the sentiment of the people and the private law of libel to deal with. When the Ku Klux outrages disgraced several of the Southern States after the military occupation of those States had ceased, there was much to be said for sending back the troops to protect the negroes and northern immigrants. But the general judgment that things ought to be allowed to take their natural course prevailed; and the result justified this policy, for the outrages after a while died out, when ordinary self-government had been restored. When recently a gigantic organization of unions of working men, purporting to unite the whole of American labour, attempted to enforce its sentences against particular firms or corporations by a boycott in which all labourers were urged to join, there was displeasure, but no panic, no call for violent remedies. The prevailing faith in liberty and in the good sense of the mass was unshaken; and the result is already justifying this tranquil faith. This tendency is not an unmixed blessing, for it sometimes allows evils to go too long unchecked. But on the whole it works for good. In giving equability to the system of government it gives steadiness and strength. It teaches the people patience, accustoming them to expect relief only by constitutional means. It confirms their faith in their institutions, as friends value one another more when their friendship has stood the test of a journey full of hardships.

IV. It is a great merit of American government that it relies very little on officials, and arms them with little power of arbitrary interference. The reader who has followed the description of Federal authorities, State authorities, county and city or township authorities, may think there is a great deal of administration; but the reason why these descriptions are necessarily so minute is because the powers of each authority are so carefully and closely restricted. It is natural to fancy that a government of the people and by the people will be led to undertake many and various functions for the people, and in the confidence of its strength will constitute itself a general philanthropic agency for their social and economic benefit. There has doubtless been of late years a tendency in this direction, a tendency to which I shall advert in a later chapter. But it has taken the direction of acting through the law rather than through the officials. That is to say, when it prescribes to the citizen a particular course of action it has relied upon the ordinary legal sanctions, instead of investing the administrative officers with inquisitorial duties or powers that it might prove oppressive, and when it has devolved active functions upon officials, they have been functions serving to aid the individual and the community rather than to interfere with or supersede the action of private enterprise. As I have dwelt on the evils which may flow from the undue application of the doctrine of direct popular sovereignty, so one must place to the credit of that doctrine and the arrangements it has dictated, the intelligence which the average native American shows in his political judgments, the strong sense he entertains of the duty of giving a vote, the spirit of alertness and enterprise, which has made him self-helpful above all other men.

V. There are no struggles between privileged and unprivileged orders, not even that perpetual strife of rich and poor which is the oldest disease of civilized states. One must not pronounce broadly that there are no classes, for in parts of the country social distinctions have begun to grow up. But for political purposes classes scarcely exist. No one of the questions which now agitate the nation is a question between rich and poor. Instead of suspicion, jealousy, and arrogance embittering the relations of classes, good feeling and kindliness reign. Everything that government, as the Americans have hitherto understood the term, can give them, the poor have already, political power, equal civil rights, a career open to all citizens alike, not to speak of that gratuitous higher as well as elementary education which on their own economic principles the United States might have abstained from giving, but which political reasons have led them to provide with so unstinting a hand. Hence the poor have had nothing to fight for, no grounds for disliking the well-to-do, no complaints to make against them. The agitation of the last few years have been directed, not against the richer classes generally, but against incorporated companies and a few individual capitalists, who have not unfrequently abused the powers which the privilege of incorporation conferred upon them, or employed their wealth to procure legislation opposed to the public interests. Where language has been used like that with which France and Germany are familiar, it has been used, not by native Americans, but by new-comers, who bring their Old World passions with them. Property is safe, because those who hold it are far more numerous than those who do not: the usual motives for revolution vanish; universal suffrage, even when vested in ignorant new-comers, can do comparatively little harm, because the masses have obtained everything which they could hope to attain except by a general pillage. And the native Americans, though the same cannot be said of some of the recent immigrants, are shrewd enough to see that the poor would suffer from such pillage no less than the rich.

A European censor may make two reflections on the way in which I have presented this part of the case. He will observe that, after all, it is no more than saying that when you have got to the bottom you can fall no farther. You may be wounded and bleeding for all that. And he will ask whether, if property is safe and contentment reigns, these advantages are not due to the economical conditions of a new and resourceful country, with an abundance of unoccupied land and mineral wealth, rather than to the democratic structure of the government. The answer to the first objection is, that the descent towards equality and democracy has involved no injury to the richer or better educated classes: to the second, that although much must doubtless be ascribed to the bounty of nature, her favours have been so used by the people as to bring about a prosperity, a general diffusion of property, an abundance of freedom of equality and of good feeling which furnish the best security against the recurrence in America of chronic Old World evils, even when her economic state shall have become less auspicious than it now is. Wealthy and powerful such a country must have been under any form of government, but the speed with which she has advanced, and the employment of the sources of wealth to diffuse comfort among millions of families, may be placed to the credit of stimulative freedom. Wholesome habits have been established among the people whose value will be found when the times of pressure approach, and though the troubles that have arisen between labour and capital may not soon pass away, the sense of human equality, the absence of offensive privileges distinguishing class from class, will make those troubles less severe than in Europe, where they are complicated by the recollection of old wrongs, by arrogance on the one side and envy on the other. . . .

VI. The government of the Republic, limited and languid in ordinary times, is capable of developing immense vigour. It can pull itself together at moments of danger, can put forth unexpected efforts, can venture on stretches of authority transcending not only ordinary practice but even ordinary law. This is the result of the unity of the nation. A divided people is a weak people, even if it obeys a monarch; a united people is doubly strong when it is democratic, for then the force of each individual will swells the collective force of the government, encourages it, relieves it from internal embarrassments. Now the American people is united at moments of national concern from two causes. One is that absence of class divisions and jealousies which has been already described. These people are homogeneous: a feeling which stirs them stirs alike rich and poor, farmers and traders, Eastern men and Western men—one may now add, Southern men also. Their patriotism has ceased to be defiant, and is conceived as the duty of promoting the greatness and happiness of their country, a greatness which, as it does not look to war or aggression, does not rebound specially, as it might in Europe, to the glory or benefit of the ruling caste or the military profession, but to that of all the citizens. The other source of unity is the tendency in democracies for the sentiment of the majority to tell upon the sentiment of a minority. That faith in the popular voice whereof I have already spoken strengthens every feeling which has once become strong, and makes it rush like a wave over the country, sweeping everything before it. I do not mean that the people become wild with excitement, for beneath their noisy demonstrations they retain their composure and shrewd view of facts. I mean only that the pervading sympathy stirs them to unwonted efforts. The steam is superheated, but the effect is seen only in the greater expansive force which it exerts. Hence a spirited executive can in critical times go forward with a courage and confidence possible only to those who know that they have a whole nation behind them. The people fall into rank at once. With that surprising gift for organization which they possess, they concentrate themselves on the immediate object; they dispense with the ordinary constitutional restrictions; they make personal sacrifices which remind one of the self-devotion of Roman citizens in the earlier and better days of Rome.

Speaking thus, I am thinking chiefly of the spirit evolved by the Civil War both in the North and South. But the sort of strength which a democratic government derives from its direct dependence on the people is seen in many smaller instances. In 1863, when on the making of a draft of men for the war, the Irish mob rose in New York City, excited by the advance of General Robert E. Lee into Pennsylvania, the State governor called out the troops, and by them restored order with a stern vigour which would have done credit to Radetzsky or Cavaignac. More than a thousand rioters were shot down, and public opinion entirely approved the slaughter. Years after the war, when the Orangemen of New York purposed to have a 12th of July procession through the streets, the Irish Catholics threatened to prevent it. The feeling of the native Americans was aroused at once; the young men of wealth came back from their mountain and seaside resorts to fill the militia regiments which were called out to guard the procession, and the display of force was so overwhelming that no disturbance followed. These Americans had no sympathy with the childish and mischievous partisanship which leads the Orangemen to perpetuate Old World feuds on New World soil. But processions were legal, and they were resolved that the law should be respected, and the spirit of disorder repressed. They would have been equally ready to protect a Roman Catholic procession.

Given an adequate occasion, executive authority is more energetic in America, more willing to take strong measures, more sure of support from the body of the people than it is in England. I may further illustrate what I mean by referring to the view which I found ordinary Americans take some eight years ago—for as to their present views I express no opinion—of the troubles of the English government and parliament in their efforts to govern Ireland. They thought that England was erring in her refusal of the demand for trenchant land legislation, and for enlarged self-government; that she would never succeed in doing everything by the imperial parliament, and through officials taken from a particular class. They held that she ought to adopt a more broadly consistent and courageous policy, ought, in fact, to grant all such self-government as might be compatible with the maintenance of ultimate imperial control and imperial unity, and ought to take the results, be they pleasant or the reverse. But they also thought that she was erring by executive leniency, that the laws ought while they stood to be more unsparingly carried out, that parliamentary obstruction ought to be more severely repressed, that any attempts at disobedience ought to be met by lead and steel. "Make good laws," they said, "but see that whatever laws you make, you enforce. At present you are doing harm both ways. You are honouring neither liberty nor authority."

VII. Democracy has not only taught the Americans how to use liberty without abusing it, and how to secure equality: it has also taught them fraternity. That word has gone out of fashion in the Old World, and no wonder, considering what was done in its name in 1793, considering also that it still figures in the programme of assassins. Nevertheless there is in the United States a sort of kindliness, a sense of human fellowship, a recognition of the duty of mutual help owed by man to man, stronger than anywhere in the Old World, and certainly stronger than in the upper or middle classes of England, France or Germany. The natural impulse of every citizen in America is to respect every other citizen, and to feel that citizenship constitutes a certain ground of respect. The idea of each man's equal rights is so fully realized that the rich or powerful man feels it no indignity to take his turn among the crowd, and does not expect any deference from the poorest. An employer of labour has, I think, a keener sense of his duty to those whom he employs than employers have in Europe. He has certainly a greater sense of responsibility for the use of his wealth. The number of gifts for benevolent and other public purposes, the number of educational, artistic, literary, and scientific foundations, is larger than even in England, the wealthiest and most liberal of European countries. Wealth is generally felt to be a trust, and exclusiveness condemned not merely as indicative of selfishness, but as a sort of offence against the public. No one, for instance, thinks of shutting up his pleasure-grounds; he seldom even builds a wall round them, but puts up low railings or a palisade, so that the sight of his trees and shrubs is enjoyed by passers-by. That any one should be permitted either by opinion or by law to seal up many square miles of beautiful mountain country against tourists or artists is to the ordinary American almost incredible. Such things are to him the marks of a land still groaning under feudal tyranny.

It may seem strange to those who know how difficult European states have generally found it to conduct negotiations with the government of the United States, and who are accustomed to read in European newspapers the defiant utterances which American politicians address from Congress to the effete monarchies of the Old World, to be told that this spirit of fraternity has its influence on international relations also. Nevertheless if we look not at the irresponsible orators, who play to the lower feelings of a section of the people, but at the general sentiment of the whole people, we shall recognize that democracy makes both for peace and for justice as between nations. Despite the admiration for military exploits which the Americans have sometimes shown, no country is at bottom more pervaded by a hatred of war, and a sense that national honour stands rooted in national fair dealing. The nation is often misrepresented by its statesmen, but although it allows them to say irritating things and advance unreasonable claims, it has not for more than forty years permitted them to abuse its enormous strength, as most European nations possessed of similar strength have in time past abused theirs.

The characteristics of the nation which I have passed in review are not due solely to democratic government, but they have been strengthened by it, and they contribute to its solidity and to the smoothness of its working. As one sometimes sees an individual man who fails in life because the different parts of his nature seem unfitted to each other, so that his action, swayed by contending influences, results in nothing definite or effective, so one sees nations whose political institutions are either in advance of or lag behind their social conditions, so that the unity of the body politic suffers, and the harmony of its movements is disturbed. America is not such a nation. It is made all of a piece; its institutions are the product of its economic and social conditions and the expressions of its character. The new wine has been poured into new bottles: or to adopt a metaphor more appropriate to the country, the vehicle has been built with a lightness, strength, and elasticity which fit it for the roads it has to traverse.